ITCH

UNCOVERING MY 30 LESSONS

IN 30 YEARS

Luke Evans

I have tried to recreate events and conversations from my memories of them. To maintain anonymity in some instances, I have changed the names of individuals and places. I may have changed some identifying characteristics and details such as physical properties, occupations and places of residence.

Any thoughts expressed on spiritual writings or theological texts are my interpretation of them and are not affiliated with or intended to be representative of any religious organizations views or ideas.

Cover design by borhan.com.au
Editing by Kevin Anderson & Associates, NY.
ISBN: 978-0-6488939-0-5

To those who chase their dreams,
and to those who have yet to find the courage to do so.
Never stop seeking your truth.

FOREWORD

PART 1 - A Modern-Day Love Story - 15 Nov, 2017

I want to share a quick story. It's about a boy who once thought he knew who he was. He had the world mapped out in his mind, and he was working through life to achieve those goals. One day, that same boy woke with a thought that he knew, deep in his heart, would change his world forever. That young man realized the reasons why his love story, amongst all of his other amazing stories in life, was not quite right. He realized that he had been looking to give his love to those that he was conditioned to feel he should. Now, this doesn't mean he didn't love those before. There was deep love in his relationships; love that he would understand more in the future. However, whether this young man realized deep down that he would end here or not, he also didn't know how to deal with it.

The journey was spiritually and emotionally tough, and it was lonely. Damn, it was lonely! In fact, it was the lowest point he had ever been in his life. The more that time passed during this period though, he understood that it was nothing to do with the person he was deciding to love, it was all to do with the perception of himself, the perception and acceptance of his family and friends, and the reality of his future that he once envisioned. A considerable part of that future was the socially conditioned expectation to find the person he loved, in true "Disney-esque" style, marry them and have a house with a white picket fence. With this new reality daunting over him, he believed he not only lost all that he identified with and the freedom to express himself in the way he felt comfortable, but he also lost his freedom to decide what he would want to see his future to be. He could no longer imagine a future with a wedding and a white picket fence if he so chose to do that. He was now choosing to be an "outcast" in his mind, based on what his society had chosen to be "right" and "wrong."

With hindsight, this same boy knows that the previous "ideal" marriage and white picket fence maybe isn't for him, well not in Disney's version of it. But the freedom to express how he loves toward the partner of his choice, and share that, legally, with his family and friends has always been a priority. For so many years, even as he realized that he would never change who he was, the freedom to marry still mattered in his heart.

In case it isn't obvious, that young boy was me. This was my story, much like many other young boys and girls across the world, who have been through their own journey for love. Some in a hugely varying degree than to others, but all in the desire to love and be loved as they see right. And today, my countrymen, the people I share my birth home with, agreed that they, too, feel that anyone can not only have the freedom to express their love for whomever they choose but, in a democratic society, they can be legally wed. This may not seem so groundbreaking after so many years of other countries already allowing this. However, this is my home country. This is the land that helped to form my own story; where the people I grew up with and were conditioned by have also agreed that it is the right thing for their fellow citizens and the future. Not just in their words, but in their laws. This is the ultimate acceptance for our current and future generations to come, in a country where love finally triumphed fear.

Today, Australia, the country where I was born and that will always be my home, told that same young boy that he cannot only be happy, but he is loved and can love in return. They gave back the freedom to choose my dreams, and that is all any person could ask.

PART 2 - A Snapshot in Time

The idea for this book came about in December 2017. It first came up on holiday, when we were on the Island of Koh Yao Noi in Thailand. The original purpose of this book was to offer young people in the gay community a new perspective on life, an alternative to the current narrative. One that was not bound by our cultural norms or societal expectations, but rather a perspective that gave another real-world example of an everyday guy who had to overcome adversity to continue on his path to a life of authenticity. I wanted to tell a story that was familiar and that would connect with many other people, but that didn't end in heartache and pain. Rather, I wanted it to be a story about requiring vulnerability and courage to remain on the path of love, growth, and hope. I am not naive enough to believe that this perspective will be universal for everyone; every person has his or her own story. Many people do not have happy endings and instead face great adversity and difficulty. But for every heartbreaking story, there are those filled with love, hope, and possibility. And my intention is to create a space where I can offer the tools I have used for those who need them; I want to show people that even if they feel they haven't been on a "hard road" relative to the struggles of others, it is still okay to tell your own story and keep seeking your authentic self. Every story matters, and our ability to share our stories with those who need to hear them matters too.

What I didn't realize is that my story would resonate with so many different people from so many different backgrounds. My intention was to share my story with other young people who identify as gay, and to explain the path I took to authenticity. I wanted to explore the struggles I faced in coming to terms with my sexuality and seeking my purpose in life, but what I have found on this journey is that my story centers around the one thing that every person seeks, regardless of background—one's authentic self. This small journey of only thirty years has made me realize that the challenges I have faced and continue to face may deal primarily with sexuality, faith, purpose, career, relationships, and so on, but they are all relevant to the one central theme of authenticity.

And as you, the reader, traverse through the pages of this book, you will find that I share my constant "itch" for more. This is a feeling, thought, or emotion familiar to people of every age, background, and walk of life. It is irrelevant to where each of us finds ourselves today whether it be emotionally, spiritually, physically, or mentally, as we all share this same desire and vision: To live a life of purpose, seek out love and belonging, and, ultimately, do so while honoring our most authentic selves.

INTRODUCTION

Ever since I was a young boy, I always recall having a feeling that I was different. A feeling that I didn't fit in with the crowd. One where I felt that I didn't meet the expectations of the world around me. A feeling deep inside of me that always felt like I was living in a world where my internal dreams and desires did not reflect how I saw all of my peers and siblings living. This never really made sense to me, but it was an underlying feeling for most of my childhood—dare I say my life. Maybe this is the challenge for many of the youth today. We all feel that we are unique, or different, or special in some sense. I never knew what the feeling stood for; I just thought that I was different. The reality of that feeling could have been numerous things—one, for instance, would be that I spent the first ten or so years of my life with acute eczema from head to toe. I was one big walking "itch." Red from the inflamed skin, allergic to pretty much everything, and in eternal misery at times, as I found it so hard to do what so many others saw so simple. It was even down to the daily reality that every time after I showered, I had to put body lotion on from head to toe, to make sure I didn't dry out crisp. The life of growing up with acute eczema didn't mean that I had a terrible childhood. Gosh, I didn't even know anything different. I just thought this was how life had to be. I mean, I hoped deep down it would change, but that was just hope.

Despite the challenges, I was still a vibrant and charismatic child. Maybe a little too charismatic, with much of my childhood spent performing in front of family crowds at their request. Memories include "line dancing" at the Jamestown show (a country town in South Australia) in my cowboy outfit with the elderly. Or, being dressed up in my mum's netball outfit—picture a young boy posing for a photo in his mother's flared, pleated skirt, old wire frame bra over top of his clothes, a player's bib, and a netball in hand—just so I could perform with my sister (or more so, as my sister's puppet). Or, continuously keeping friends and family entertained on our weekend trips away with silly banter, dance routines, and lousy magic tricks. It wasn't all that bad, it was just a time filled with unknowns and a lingering illness that we couldn't quite manage to beat.

My mum had spent most of these years dealing with all the new and unusual issues that came up, ensuring that I had the best care every day, and trying to seek the best solution for her child to live a relatively "normal" life. Everything from steroid-based lotions (which seemed to work the best at relieving the symptoms, but did nothing for the cause), all the way to drinking Chinese herbal medicines (which looked and tasted like what a child could only describe as "crap"), getting "past life" healings in spiritualist groups, to the one thing that I have to admit in my formative years I still stand by, which is kinesiology. For those who don't know, kinesiology is the study of the mechanics of body movement (at its most basic form). It is used in many different forms, depending on the practitioner. When it came to this practice, what I found the most success with was when we used it to talk, not to me, but to my body, to find out what was aggravating it so much internally. The one thing I learned then, which has continued into my formative and adult years, is that the symptom is simply that—a symptom—and that we need to always delve deeper into our bodies to find the cause if we want true change to take place. Diagnose the "DIS-ease," and you are on the path to solve the issue.

Now, I could go on for a long time with this topic, to talk about all the difficulties that took place in my life in those first ten years. Painful experiences from hospital visits to near-death experiences from drugs that were meant to "help" me. I recall when I was quite young, maybe five or six, and I had contracted a throat infection due to a low immune system and, quite likely, the annual flu season that takes place in your small country towns. For most people, a throat infection would be treatable. Unfortunately, when you have such a low immune system and broken skin that is susceptible to infection, a throat infection can turn ugly. I must have been coughing a lot from the infection in my throat, and without thinking, scratched my skin and spread the bacteria from my throat onto my skin. This small act, coupled with a low immune system, saw me go from a sore throat to a body covered in staph infection. The result was red, swollen skin covered in a collection of sores filled with pus. Delightful, right? Another such event, which also started with a throat infection, occurred a year or two later in Adelaide, South Australia. I had been unwell from my throat, and my skin would naturally react and flare up due to being so run down. As I was in such a bad way, my mum took me to a specialist to be treated. He gave me a shot of penicillin to stop the infection. At this stage, we weren't aware that I was allergic to penicillin, despite being allergic to almost everything. Overnight, in response to the shot, my body reacted and my throat began to close up and I couldn't breathe. My mum woke to me coughing uncontrollably and she freaked out. She threw me into the car and did 160 km/hr through every red light to get me to the nearest hospital. Needless to say, I survived, but it was quite the ordeal. However, as scary as it may sound in hindsight, it was sadly just another day when it came to my health. No matter what we did, it seemed to just be one challenge after another.

I had allergies, childhood torment, and feelings of looking like a "freak" (still one of the vilest words in the English language). I missed opportunities like participating in school sports days or swimming in the Great Barrier Reef on our family holiday, as I wasn't well enough (be that in body or mind). I had restless nights filled with so much scratching. Oh God, if I could say one thing I do not miss, it's the scratching. There was this constant itch that riddled my body from head to toe, day and night. So much so, that for most of the time, I didn't even know I was scratching. It was just happening. A physical reaction to a deep urge of being unsettled.

Over the years though, there is another "itch" I have come to realize has not disappeared. An "itch" that has developed as part of my mechanism to understand the universe and find my way through life. Today, I don't have anything wrong with my skin. After years of pain and difficulty, we found a way to calm down my body internally by the age of ten, and through a focus on health I have managed to keep myself healthy ever since. But I have decided this "itch," this deep desire or urge that forces a physical reaction, is not just under the surface of my skin, it is in all aspects of life. Whether the "itch" was to travel, learn, change jobs, meet new people, be promiscuous, be courageous, be daring—it doesn't matter. This "itch" was an inherent desire that I had learned to listen to, and rather than scratch it to make it go away, I used it to do what I did as a child: use it to understand what my body or my soul is telling me.

Without even knowing it, this same mechanism is what has driven me through my last thirty years. From moving to London at the age of eighteen with a desire to travel and see the world, to changing jobs from a high-paying corporate role one day to being a travel agent the next; from living and working in rural Nepal, to volunteer work that took me from Australia to South Africa. From having the courage to accept my sexuality despite it being against the "norm," to moving countries and living abroad now for the last five years... These all started with an "itch" that began deep inside, teeming with a desire for more than what I felt I had. An "itch" to explore the world around me, to expand beyond my personal comfort zone, and to seek more meaning from my life. And for most people, we feel this same "itch" in our lives. This deep seated desire for more. Something that may challenge us, activate fear within our bodies, offer a vision of a life that we believe we could only ever dream of, or show us the best versions of ourselves—just to wake up at that moment, scratch that "itch" without thought, and get back to our daily grind. This same feeling can be likened to the Universe, God, or even your future self, offering you an idea or insight into where your path should be leading. It is the signpost, the message, the gut feeling that each of us either choose to follow or that we should follow more in order to stay on the path to our most authentic selves.

This book is the story of my last thirty years, and how listening to that "itch," and acting upon it, has taken me on an extraordinary journey of self-discovery, love, and service. It has been integral in creating the reality I have now and in the most recent years deciding what type of future I want. A future that many of us start to question and challenge at the age of thirty, an age when significant internal change takes place, priorities shift, and social frameworks are either tested or chosen.

It is also a time when I have undergone a major reflection on the life I have led to this point, and I have tried to make sense of the experiences I've had and the lessons I've learned. For so many years, I would try to make sense of what I was doing, why I was doing it, and how I could get closer to doing all of the things I felt I "should" have been doing. I recall so many times in my life when I felt so lost. I felt like I wasn't on track or achieving anything but was instead forcing myself to do what I thought I was supposed to be doing. I didn't understand that life is a constant dance, a teeming space of energy which ebbs and flows in the direction you need to go, not where you think you should go. By understanding these lessons, I believe I am able to better understand why I am standing where I am today, and I am able to have a more complete view of where I want to go in the future. As a man who identifies as gay, it is also a time within my community, where many of us look to the past and to the present to see what our peers are doing and how they, too, are spending their days. As social creatures, we use these societal frameworks to understand our place, our opportunities, our limitations, and our potential future. But it also means that we have a huge responsibility to one another to ensure we are doing all we can to create healthy and prosperous lives to which we can aspire.

This story doesn't have a final ending or outcome, and it doesn't show you the only way to live your life. What it does offer is a different perspective, one where I have recounted my most memorable or impactful experiences, and I imagine what my life would look like now if I had written to my younger self and offered some insight about what to expect, what to embrace, and what to avoid. These reflections are my thirty lessons in thirty years. Whether it relates to relationships, career, sex, or soul, I give you an account of what has given me a life, which if I was to leave this world tomorrow, I know I did all I can to make it an incredible one. This is also a reflection on what I may have done differently if I had the chance to do it all over again. An experience where I began with an "itch" that caused deep pain and sadness in my world, but where I learned to master it and listen to it, to understand what the universe wants me to learn and lead a life of purpose. At the same time, using these lessons, I offer you a new perspective on the future. Regardless of the community to which you belong, we have an opportunity to avoid the social expectations defined by our peers and to create lives that truly matter to each of us, individually. Whether your community tells you that you must get married, have children, and settle down by thirty, or that you should be living a life of partying, sex, drugs, and fabulousness, these expectations no longer matter. In fact, they never did. That was just our perception. What I have learned is that all that matters is that which resonates deep within us.

So, come with me on this journey, open your hearts and minds, and see if you find an "itch" that may lead you to your greatest self.

PART ONE –
HELLO, I AM LUKE

Born on the 29th of February, 1988, in Adelaide, South Australia; in a loving working-class family; the youngest of four. I spent most of my childhood in rural South Australia and then Northern Queensland. As a young boy growing up in the country in a town of two thousand people, with a wilder imagination than Walt Disney, I imagined that one day I would be one of the world's greatest archaeologists, exploring the world for ancient artifacts and dinosaur bones from millions of years ago. I also thought it possible that one day I could be a secret agent engaging in covert operations, or a famous Hollywood actor. Never did I think that this same boy would one day find himself living in the Middle East, running his own business, and developing a deep passion for travel and people.

As I mentioned earlier, the first ten years of my life I spent battling acute eczema. This condition was a long battle and meant that my family had to deal with quite a sick child for most of those ten years. Despite speaking casually about it now, for so many years all I wanted most was to hide away from the world and not be seen. All I dreamt about was staying in my room, or having the house to myself, so I could play and express myself in ways that I wouldn't be judged or given awkward or pitiful looks. The effects of this playing carried into my adult life, where even now, I find myself battling with internal dialogue about my physical state: Am I strong enough? Do I look fit enough? Will people judge how I look? Each day, however, I get a little stronger and more confident with who I am, and what I have to offer. And these battles, these years of physical pain and scarring (quite literally), taught me some of my most important lessons in life. In many ways, with hindsight, these things along with all the love and care my mother gave me during this time, set me up for the person I am today.

By the time I was twelve years old my skin condition had subsided, after years of trying every remedy known to man—even those known only to the spirit world! From steroids for the skin to ancient herbal remedies, kinesiology, and "past life" work—when I say everything, I mean it. Eventually, we found a way to cool my body from the inside using herbal remedies, kinesiology, and some spiritual work, all of which began to heal my tired body slowly. By this stage, our world had changed, and my family had split. My mum and dad could no longer be together, and so we dealt with their divorce. Divorce is a messy thing and it, unfortunately, brings the worst out in people. Given my years spent with my mum, and due to my dad's work schedule, we stayed with her.

After they were divorced, we went from living quite comfortably— medium to high income earnings, large house, full fridge, abundance of presents over the holiday period, entertainment consoles, annual family holidays... all the things you care about as a child and which I am grateful for, as that financial support helped during so many years of "dis-ease"—to living day-to-day in terms of finances. My mother was earning minimum wage, and raising two teenage children on her own (as my older brothers were already out of the home), with no consistent support from my dad. This made for some tough times, more so for my mother, who although she struggled to know if she could put food on the table that night, always gave us a house that was clean, safe, and full of love and support. We never went without the basics, but it did teach us at an early age what it meant to work for what you want. This saw me start casual work outside of school from the age of fourteen, and I wouldn't have it any other way. The earliest and best piece of advice I have ever had from my mother was, "If you want something, you need to work for it."

Aside from work, my creativity and imagination gave me a reprieve in what is always a tumultuous and confusing time in every person's life. I mean, teenage years are hard enough without losing the family structure you once knew. I found myself feeling low and in difficult emotional states. Even though I knew it was a good thing my parents weren't together, it still impacted the dynamics of the house, the stress on my mum, and the reality that I had a different set of responsibilities weighing on my shoulders than I had before. To try and cope with these changes, and in hindsight, without even really being conscious of the decision, I turned to acting. And I was quite good at it too! Before this, I would go to Choi Kwon Do classes, or play hockey at school. This concept of organized sport was never my strength, but I did it to fit in. At the same time at school, I was always part of some creative outlet, but I wouldn't focus on it. For some reason though, this type of break in my world demanded I move into a performing art to cope. There was something about putting on a costume, or even just getting into character that allowed me to emotionally and mentally detach from my own world that I was struggling to understand, and to take on someone else's. Whether that new character was from the depths of my own imagination, or one that was written for me, the act of quite literally putting your own character to one side and taking form in another was therapeutic. And this newfound love of acting saw me get involved with a range of different organizations and pursue the world of the stage. I performed in major theater productions, from primary school performances to high school musicals. I was even asked to play the lead role in the Townsville City Christmas Carols and sing with Julie Anthony. In South Australia, I was part of the "elite ensemble" at an acting school and casting agency called Actors Ink, where I was put forward for roles in movies, radio adverts, and TV shows. This experience included an Australian favorite, *McLeod's Daughters*—in which I played the punk boyfriend from the city, for the character Rose. Hilarious. A demanding role where I ended up showcasing my fantastic talent through, wait for it, a photo of me in the show. This was not quite the lead role, or even the speaking role every aspiring actor would dream about, but it was something. However, jokes aside, this outlet of acting served me well from age eleven until I was seventeen. It gave me hope and escape. It gave me an outlet to express myself while being able to create experiences for other people. It gave me reprieve from a world that felt too difficult at times. And it was my first taste of using creativity as service to the world.

At the age of sixteen, I moved to Brisbane from Adelaide, where I had been living for the past year with my dad. I decided that I wanted to try living with him and his new family for a change, and to give me a closer connection to him. Sadly, it wasn't quite the move I had in mind. Despite being a loving and kind man, his most dangerous vice, alcohol, had gotten the better of him. It was a tough year of growth for me, one of the lowest points I have seen for my dad, and a lesson that the grass is definitely not always greener. Once in Brisbane and back with my mum and sister, a new road began for me. It saw me graduate from high school and pursue a desire to explore the world. In many ways, this was the beginning of my many "itches" to come. It was the start of something so magnificent, yet so subtle in its approach that a young Luke could never comprehend or understand.

This is where the major lessons in my life began.

SEEKING MORE AUTHENTIC LOVE

It was 2003, I was sixteen, and I had just moved to Brisbane after leaving Adelaide, where I'd lived for the last year with my dad, his partner, and her children. The move was made a year earlier in the hope that I would enjoy life down there, rather than in Townsville, where my mum was in a challenging relationship of her own at the time. As I learned, it doesn't matter who you are, we are all here to learn something—no one is perfect, not even our parents. I recall coming back from a holiday with my dad, and I had an "itch" to move down there ASAP. My mum was a little heartbroken, but my dad was excited. Before I knew it, I packed up and moved to Adelaide, dreaming of what any fifteen-year-old boy would want: Good school life, comfortable home life, fun parties, cool job, and a girlfriend. I managed to find most of those things, although I always hated school no matter where I went!

Unfortunately—or perhaps fortunately—the universe had plenty in store for me to learn during that year. It was a time of super highs and some extreme lows; a rough year, to say the least, but I don't look back on it with a heavy heart. I look back and see it as a year of learning and growth. Without that year, my soul would not have been capable of learning what it did and finding ways to use that knowledge in the future for even more depth and understanding. So with those life-changing experiences packed up, and not yet unraveled from my past year, I found myself, quite literally, heading to Brisbane overnight. Yes, the "itch" to leave that place, as quickly as I arrived, was real. And before I knew it, I was in a new city, at a new school, with new people, and now, with a potential new relationship ahead of me.

It was in my first few weeks of moving to a new school in Brisbane that I met this confident, creative, and gorgeous girl, who walked up to me and introduced herself into my life. It was nearing the end of the school day, in the last period, when I was walking from the canteen area along the driveway next to our main assembly hall, to our drama room that was hidden beneath the hall. Large trees, very quintessentially Australian, also ran along the side of the hall. The driveway I was on was steep and led down to our large grass sporting fields, which lie between the suburban dwellings of inner-city Brisbane. Everything was still quite new to me, including the formal school attire I had to wear: white, short-sleeved shirt, tie, grey pleated school shorts, long woolen socks to our knees, and black leather shoes. When it was cold, we had a woolen pullover that we could also wear. This was a far cry from my usual public school attire that I was used to—shorts, t-shirt, and sport shoes, at best.

As I approached the drama class, veering off the steep driveway to the steps that led down to the dark classroom, I saw this charismatic and good-looking blonde girl standing by the wooden bag racks. She was chatting with her friend Ashley when I arrived. She didn't seem to be the "popular girl" as such, but she was certainly known by everyone and seemed to be in her zone in that space. Seeing I was the new boy and didn't have many friends, I guess I looked like an easy target to approach.

When we did lock eyes and she made her way over to me, it was like one of those movie scenes, where the boy meets the girl for the first time, doves fly from behind them and music plays in the background. Ok, maybe not that dramatic, but it was significant. As she approached me, without what I would normally expect as a "dare" from her friends, she said, "Hi, I'm Karley, and you're cute." Charming, right! It still makes me smile. At the time though, I had never come across this type of confidence before and I was a little taken back. I didn't know whether to be charmed or scared. Something told me to hold onto the former. Naturally, I just smiled and said, "Hi, I'm Luke."

I could say, "and the rest was history," but that would lose all the good bits. It wasn't as easy as it sounds. We had quite a tumultuous relationship. As any high school relationship can go, we were on again, off again. One minute we were riding high, the next we were archenemies (which would usually only last a few days). And ultimately, as relationships at such a young age go, we were destined to be "together forever"—although, of course, we most certainly were not. There was something about her though, and I felt the "itch" to learn more from the first day we met when the universe thrust her upon me.

Her personality was vibrant and eccentric, which shone through in her passion for creative arts. Everything from singing to dancing and acting. But most importantly to a sixteen-year-old boy, she was "hot." There was no doubt about that, and it was what drew a lot of attention for her over the years. Without knowing it, her creative streak is what really drew my attention. I have always been an artistic type myself. At times, I rejected it, as my perception of creativity was that it wasn't masculine enough. Creative energy is infectious, energizing, and refreshing. It gives life to the imagination and takes you far from the world that you know. At times, it was a great escape, and other times it was just hilarious to explore. Either way, she had this ability, and it drew me in.

But the one thing I always loved was that she had this beautiful sense of vulnerability, and a more profound understanding of spirituality, similar to my own, that resonated the most with me. There was something really attractive in seeing someone who was all these physical things—pretty, funny, witty—but at the same time, below that layer of outward identity, had a real connection with a deeper self.

Now, this girl didn't have the most astounding reputation at school, and that was in most part because she owned her character. She didn't quite fit with the "cool" kids, but she was not an outcast. I guess she was just another performing-arts child who didn't have time for anything between school, acting, dancing, singing, and every other performing art she tried to fit into her schedule. I became captivated from the moment we met. There was something about her. I used to think that it must have been that smile, or that body, I couldn't tell. But we both instantly became infatuated with one another. We would chat until all hours of the night on the phone, hang out away from school any chance that we would get, and find ways to catch up in the school yard. We didn't have an openly affectionate relationship at school, as we did sit with different crowds, but the moment we were alone, it was like no one else mattered.

As I said, over time, I learned what drew me to her the most; it was that deeper spiritual connection we had with one another. You may or may not have heard the term before, but it was like when we met, we both knew we had a contract with one another—a deeper spiritual agreement to connect and learn from each other. I remember so distinctly to this day that first meeting. I remember how I was still feeling so new to the school and uncertain about who everyone was and who I should be friends with; I remember standing at the bottom of those steps at school near the drama room—it was a warm, humid afternoon, slightly overcast, the end of a QLD summer day. I remember her sweet perfume she wore, her uniform which was a bit scruffy after a full day at school, the soft touch of her hand as she grabbed mine. It was all so new, but it was almost familiar. It was like we knew each other, but were meeting in our new human bodies for the first time. It was almost comical, with hindsight. It's like two actors greeting each other on stage as if they never met before.

Over the years, we both challenged each other and were quite emotional about most things. I mean, what else do you expect from a high school love affair. I found myself falling quickly for this new girl as she brought energy into my life that I was missing. She showed me things about myself that I didn't see at the time—especially when it came to my creativity. But mostly, she showed me that I could be myself without fear of being judged. We both had histories and we both suffered to fit in at times, but together the world was OK. At this stage, she was my first love. She was the first person I had sex with, and she was the first real girlfriend I brought home to my family and who they also befriended. Don't get me wrong, I had plenty of girl "friends," but never intimately. I managed to get girlfriends over the years, but I wasn't overly confident with myself— despite the confidence others had in both my looks and personality—and I didn't quite understand what all the fuss was about when it came to dating.

Our relationship lasted from 2003 when I met her in Grade 11, all the way until around 2008, when we were both back and forth to Australia between time living overseas. Throughout that time we were on and off—partly due to our physical distance, but also due to the fact that we couldn't seem to keep our relationship together. Somehow our relationship got stronger over time, but I still felt like we were ships in the night moving away from each other. As I have said, when we were together, it was like nothing else mattered, but even in the depths of that young love, I still didn't feel like I was settled enough with myself. The on and off was mainly due to me. I would come up with a range of excuses as to why we couldn't be together. Everything from being hurt by fights we had, to her choice of the work she did after school—which found her working in nightclubs until the early hours of the morning, when I wouldn't even go out to clubs. I just felt like we had had our time together and I needed to move on. But I could never figure out where I needed to go! It was like the moment I broke up with her, I would feel even more lost and I didn't have the luck I thought I would with the ladies. I would think, *Surely there was a part of me that was ready to be a crazy twentysomething who goes out and meets girls, has fun, shags around, and is a real boy's-boy (you know, how we are all expected to be within our macho Australian male culture).* But no matter how much I tried to find this side of me, it never worked. So I would go back to what I knew, which was the love of this amazing girl. However, as I wasn't being true to myself and this behavior wasn't sustainable or healthy, over time, our relationship began to break down.

By the time I was twenty-two, our relationship had come to an end. I remember breaking up with her and leaving her house (it may not have been the last time, but it was the time when I knew it was truly over). I was driving home, trying to hold it together, hurting and angry, not able to make sense of the world ahead. Feeling lost and vulnerable, I ended up working myself into such a state that I had to pull the car over and call my mum. Heartbroken and lost, filled with anxiety, I bawled my eyes out on the phone.

"I loved her though, Mum," I cried. "Why couldn't it work? Why couldn't we have stayed together? Surely we were meant to be?" Ain't young love grand! At that stage, I truly believed that this was one of the hardest things I would ever have to deal with in my life. The break of a "love" that defined me, that was part of my world, and that I could no longer try and control. I had to let it go. I had to let go of this person that everyone told me was going to be my "forever."

As I look back though, I know that the biggest trial of this relationship was not the fact that she was my first love. That mattered, but it wasn't what hurt the most. It was the uncertainty and identity dissonance that was going on inside of me. This girl represented everything I was trying so hard to be. I was trying to be what I would have called a "normal" twenty-year-old guy, living a good life with his super talented and good-looking girlfriend. And by normal, I mean, I was forcing myself to live this heteronormative life that I felt everyone wanted me to live. Little did I know, at this stage, that this is how I was truly feeling. But, what I knew for sure was that the break of this relationship meant one step closer to finding out whatever it was I felt I was looking for.

It was the step toward the unknown, leaving behind the Luke I felt I was trying to be and stepping into the next stage of my life without the anxiety of this apparent charade. And when I look around me now, I see so many people who look to be in that same situation. Forcing themselves to be with someone that they believe they are "meant" to be with, creating drama and heartache in their life, and blaming everything outside of the fact that they simply are not happy. I did not know why I was truly unhappy, I just knew I always felt not enough for this girl. She deserved this guy I was trying to be, but the issue was that I was simply trying too hard to be it.

As I look back on this story in my life, I see that the "itch" I felt was this desire to explore myself in a more full and authentic way. At the time, this made no sense to me and in so many ways I avoided this feeling, as I knew that it would lead to the inevitable—breakup and heartbreak. But if I had the tools and foresight, I would've seen that I had a deeper need to understand love and even bigger void of not being enough for her.

The main lesson that I took from this experience was **do not hold life hostage to change**. I had to learn to allow change to take place without forcing my expectation on it. I had to allow myself to feel these changes, and trust that the love I feel is true, but its future may not look as I feel it should. But this, too, is ok. I had to trust in that, and know that the more I resist, it will persist.

The perfect analogy for this is that of the sailing boat. Imagine we go through life on a sailing boat. This boat at times runs perfectly along the water, with the wind in the sails. It makes for a smooth ride and life can feel on track. All of sudden though, the wind begins to change, the boat starts to hit up against the opposing streams of air and the water starts to turn choppy. Your boat is no longer sailing smoothly, but you are fixated on the original path and direction. You have two options in this moment: shift your mast and move with the new wind direction, or continue to fight against the changing tides. Life can be just like this, and this lesson was the first and certainly not the last reminder of this analogy. I could either choose to keep fighting against the changing weather and batter my boat along the way, or I could accept that I need the winds and that they will guide me in the right path for safety. If I just shift the mast slightly, I will move direction, which may not be in the original direction I thought best, but I will fall out of the battling winds against me and suddenly collect that energy to propel me forward.

This experience, whilst I was still only young, was transformative and the first of the major "wind changes" in life that would shift my direction and lead me to the path of a more authentic understanding of love.

GLOBAL CONNECTION

When I was seventeen and about to finish school, many of my friends were looking for the right university to go to so they could continue studying and become something significant in the world. I, on the other hand, would sit in the classroom at school and daydream while staring out the window, which looked out over the football oval toward the city. I would think about what marvelous and wondrous things must be lying out there waiting for me. The thought of going to another institution gave me immediate anxiety! I just wasn't built that way. Instead, I had my sights set on something far greater. One night, my best mate Beth and I were out back of my house in Brisbane, lying in an empty blow-up pool, talking about what we were going to do the following year. We both had no real idea.

Beth and I were very close. I had met her at school and we'd had an immediate connection. She was a fun, bubbly girl who was the epitome of a loyal friend. The bond we shared was unique and went beyond a normal high school friendship. She always did well at school and was part of the prefect team; she was friends with most people and was well liked. But she also battled with her weight and was the subject of the usual taunts in the schoolyard. But I had her back no matter what. I recall a not-so-kind interaction she had with a girl in our drama class, in which a rather vicious side of me came out in defense of my friend. Since the beginning, I felt connected to Beth and her family so the idea of making plans together was a given.

Beth was considering university but wasn't excited about the idea either. As we spoke more about our future, travel was on my mind. To be honest, I had never even left Australia at that point, al- though I had done some travel interstate throughout my childhood. But the idea of travel always resonated with me, even when I couldn't understand it. In this same conversation, Beth casually mentioned that her cousin Renee was living in London. She made a comment, which I am sure was in jest, that we could always go and see her. Bingo! And just like that, I had my next big "itch": London, here we come!

I still remember what it was like when I landed in London, after our transit experience in Seoul, South Korea; everything felt so foreign. Almost the type of remote feeling that I would expect if I entered another planet. It was surreal. I recall getting off the Tube in Clapham Common and walking out in the main street. I was overwhelmed with where I was. The houses were these small, funny-shaped buildings, built side by side and running the full length of the streets. The roads were busy and people were everywhere. Despite Brisbane being the capital city, it still felt like a large country town at times, and at that moment it was nothing compared to where I found myself standing. The energy was electric, the noises and smells were different, and without expecting it, I suddenly felt like Alice who had fallen down the rabbit hole. I remember I used to wake up during our first week, go up to the second floor of the flat where we lived in Clapham, which had a window that looked out across the rooftops, and I'd open it up and just stare at life going past. It was like I was in a real-life movie with red double-decker buses and everything! *This experience is so much bigger than what any university textbook would have taught me*, I thought.

When we were in the UK, it was all about working to live! We had a small amount of savings, and so I needed to find work quickly. We tried living in the countryside (after sheer desperation for employment) and quit within a week of moving there. Once back in London, we decided to be a little more creative with our work options for us to stay in the city. The pressure of trying to get work and the time it took to make it happen tested us! I remember calling my mum in tears, saying that I don't understand why I did this; it was a stupid idea; I shouldn't have left home. I think I even said, "I would rather just come back home, go to university, live with you (which I hadn't done for a couple of years by that point), and just get a job at McDonald's. All of my friends are doing that, why the hell am I trying to do so much more?" My mum consoled me, despite it killing her to hear me so upset, and she told me just to give it a little longer and be strong. I hung up, in tears, depressed, and feeling like I was over the whole experience. Fifteen minutes after that call, a temp agency I was in touch with called me back and offered me a role at an engineering company, in their HR/Recruitment department. What a relief! And little did I know that this role would take me through my entire time in London.

When I was seeking work in London, I recall I even went as far as applying for a job as cabin crew for EasyJet! Hilarious. I was accepted and went for the interview and assessment days and made it through with flying colors (no pun intended), and they even sent me an offer letter. I forgot this experience over time as, again, it felt so foreign. I mean, I didn't even think I would look at a cabin crew job in my life, but here I was, with no clue as to how I applied for it in the first place, but having the courage to show up for it anyway. Once I came to my senses, I declined and got back on with the work I was doing. I still wonder where life would have taken me if I had accepted that role. Would I have remained in the UK until now? Would I have gone elsewhere? Would I have been exposed to the gay world and have "come out" earlier? It's amazing how the universe will offer us multiple paths, and what we use to decide on the "right" one for us.

Initially, when I started with this engineering company, I was offered the role as a temporary position for a few weeks to clear a backlog of admin tasks. *Easy enough*, I thought. I went in each day and sorted through the spreadsheets and paperwork that had backed up over the last year. It was mundane work, but I was glad to be earning a wage and sharing an office with some kind people. I learned plenty of small lessons throughout this experience. Lessons like, don't sit and listen to music at your desk without asking, as it is apparently not ok in an office space. Make sure you are seen to be doing the work you're assigned and don't sit on MySpace or email friends. And never be seen to be too quick at completing your work if you are only temp staff. Unfortunately, I hadn't quite gotten that last one under my belt, and one day I promptly told them that I had completed all the work that I was assigned. Surprised, the manager thanked me and said I could leave early that day if I liked. Any person would jump at this, but for some reason, something inside of me thought that I might not be coming back if I did that—I mean, the work was complete. So instead, I found some courage within and I declined to leave early, in the assumption that, inevitably, there would be more work for me to do. Anything. It didn't even have to be this same type of work.

Thankfully for me, this offer seemed to have gone well. In no time, and in addition to the work I had been doing, I was now working with the recruitment team, managing graduate inductions and even liaising with hotels for recruits to ensure their welcome packages had arrived. Phew! This timely insight seemed to have saved me from looking for another job and gave me work that, to this day, was beneficial experience in the workplace. But it also gave me access to people from all over the world. I was not only an eighteen-year-old working in a major city that was a twenty-two-hour flight from my hometown, but I was doing business with people from all over the globe. That same young boy who was only in English class dreaming of the world from suburban Australia under two years ago, was now sitting in his office in

Chiswick, working with a team of professionals and expanding his life in one of the most international cities in the world. This somewhat trivial work was my first real experience of seeing a significant dream come to reality.

This desire to travel the world came from my original dreams for a life that was filled with global connections. I recall even before I was sitting in class dreaming, I used to tell my dad and his partner in Adelaide that I would one day work on cruise ships or airlines just so I could go and explore the world. It was as if some part of me knew that this was destined for my future. This desire was activated for me as I felt limited in my Australian surroundings. Traveling abroad not only took care of my desire to see the world, but it connected me with people from around the globe. It showed this boy who once lived in a country town of two thousand people, that there are people all over this earth living lives that are so different to what I understood life to be. It opened my eyes and it taught me a significant lesson of **courage.** This courage would only take a few moments to put into action, but it would turn a situation away from something that could be riddled with fear into moments of sheer bravery instead. If I had not taken that leap of faith in the first place to follow my "itch" to travel overseas and reject the normal path to higher education at that time, despite all the challenges that I could be facing ahead, I would never have had the opportunity to see the world in a way far different to many of my peers at home.

This period of my life also taught me one other integral and ongoing lesson in life—***Trust that something far greater than you —God, the universe—has your back.*** We all speak about how much we trust in God or the universe to do what is right by us, but without knowing it, this experience was the beginning of learning a really important spiritual lesson in life. If we truly believe in a higher force beyond ourselves, and we believe that it has assisted us to get to where we stand today, then why is it in moments of fear or uncertainty, we believe that now is the time that it won't support us? Why is it that in moments that call for courage and bravery, our mind switches to scarcity and fear? For me, I am still truly learning this in my life even now. But as I look back and reflect on my path, I can see that this was one of my first lessons in really trusting something beyond myself.

This experience was the beginning of my international adventures, the first taste of life abroad, and the start of my immersion into the global community that we all call home.

A MATERIAL WORLD

After my time in London, and traveling throughout Europe, I was broke and in need of some work. I had this "itch" by the end of my time in Europe where I thought that I would come back to Australia, settle down for a bit, and start to focus on my career path. As much as I wanted to explore the world, I was lacking in direction and needed to work on my material successes.

It was 2008, I was back, and I couldn't believe how much I had changed over the time I was away. The world I once knew looked different. The things that once entertained me now felt monotonous, and life didn't have that same shine to which I had become accustomed. Through my sister, I managed to get an interview with the expanding private banking department of the Bank of Queensland. Given my experience and customer service background, they were eager for some fresh blood in the department. Again, I had no desire to be in banking necessarily, but at that age, I was happy to go where the opportunities and money were.

Private banking was the perfect job for someone seeking material successes and a strong corporate path. It offered great money, perks in the world of finance, and showed me that hard work would be rewarded. It was my first exposure to an actual corporate environment, and I was immediately dealing with high net-worth individuals, the amazing lives some of them led, and the not-so-fabulous lives of others, though there is something to be said about maintaining good face. During my time in this role, I learned about the power of money in the world, despite not truly understanding it for myself, and the importance of routine. I also learned about the value of relationships, especially in the world of business. I remember thinking, *I am twenty-one years of age and funding loans for more than I've earned in my lifetime!* However, these people trusted us and the work that we did. Over time, I also learned that the stronger our relationships were, the more natural and enjoyable our jobs became.

However, no matter how hard I tried, I was struggling to fall into the work. I looked around at my peers and I saw others handing themselves over to the work. I felt that I was almost doing the same, but I had no clue what I was doing half the time as I didn't have a background in this field. I recall my general manager pulling me aside one time for a one-to-one. He told me that I was doing a great job, and had some amazing potential for the department. He also said that I had to work on my approach, as I was currently resembling a bull in a china shop. To which I thought, *I may be lacking in finesse but I am certainly getting the work done, nonetheless.*

As time went on I could see the potential and reward of hard work in this corporate environment, but I fought with the deep desire for soul-satisfying work, and was wary of aligning myself with the fat pigs of greed and self-indulgence. I liked how it made me feel at the start, to be working toward this material success that I thought I was seeking, but over time that focus shifted and I started spending my weekends volunteering at the local children's hospital, reading spiritual self-help books, and seeking something that would give my soul far greater reward than what I was getting from my job.

Despite starting out with this "itch" for my career, I could feel another showing itself at the same time. This was a deeper desire for a more meaningful pathway to my work. I was finding that I could walk the walk, talk the talk, and looked great in a suit, but I was so bored and unfulfilled that it was starting to wear me down. At this stage of my life, I had been quite a spiritual bypass—seeking meaning in a few self-help books and getting involved in some local social programs. But I wanted something more. Maybe this initial "itch" to chase my career path was too simple, and I needed to get back to studying and find a more meaningful pathway through education.

One of my best mates, Linda, who I had met in Turkey in 2007 and who I remained friends with since, was a social worker and had always encouraged me to look into a more meaningful work path. Linda and I were polar opposites in so many ways, but we connected during a time when we were both seeking more from the world. Linda had grown up in rural Victoria, a small town outside of Melbourne in Australia, and had been living for a year or two in London when we met. The story of our meeting is quite funny. We were both on a tour of Turkey in April, which was for Anzac Day commemorations, which is the Australian and New Zealand Army Corps.

We hadn't quite spoken before the stay in Anzac Cove, but on one of the following nights after (of our seven-night stay) we were all having drinks in the hotel. Things were getting a bit out of hand and I found myself sitting with this woman chatting about the trip and life in general. We were interrupted while talking and I had to leave the conversation for a bit. We laugh at the next part, as I said to her, "Sorry, I just have to go over here. But don't worry, I will be back." Such an odd thing to say, but obviously made an impact, as eleven years later we are still friends.

During this time in my life, I had just returned from London and so had she, but was living in Melbourne again. I told her of my dilemma and that I wanted to study something formally, as I thought that would help with this "itch" for a more meaningful pathway. She suggested social work, given my strong interest in social action and personal development. I thought it was a great idea. Well, until I realized that I had to work all day in the bank, to then come home and continue studying each night until late in my room. What type of life was this? What became clear quite quickly was that whilst I had these urges to seek material success through work and find a clear career pathway, and then find a more meaningful pathway through higher education, I was simply acting on the impulse and not allowing this "itch" to translate over time into something that also held meaning for me. It seems that I was allowing these ideas to be translated without too much thought and still remain opposite to one another. Greedy banker by day, studious and action-driven social worker by night.

Needless to say, after six months of study, I decided that I was not cut out for both of these, and naturally material comfort and corporate pursuit of happiness won over four years of formal education. I had received distinctions and high distinctions in my marks for university for that first semester, but that wasn't enough reason for me to continue. My banking job went on for a few months longer, until I realized that I not only didn't want to study, I also didn't want to be so serious with work. I couldn't find my feet and I couldn't make sense of what I kept feeling, but instead of sitting in a space of unhappiness, I changed my ideas and looked for the next adventure.

During this time in my life, it seems that I had two different "itches" playing out in my mind. One for material comfort, the other for more meaning. You could almost say it was the Ego and the Soul battling it out for the win. This same battle continued on as a theme in my life for some time. I found myself trying to make sense of my role, my purpose, and how I could follow this path I feel is set out for me. Little did I realize at this stage in my life that this was in fact the exact path I was meant to be on. The experience in the corporate world was the beginning of my required work experience in life, and the study I undertook wouldn't be the last time that I battled with the idea that I require some type of formal education. My lack of direction and lack of knowledge led me closer to my most authentic path, I just simply couldn't make sense of it. I would find myself feeling really down about what I was doing, lost in between the worlds of ego and soul work, and constantly feeling like I had to make sense of what it looked like for me. On one hand I gained work experience for the future and found that I had the right passion, but maybe the wrong direction. On the other hand, I was working without joy and reminded myself that formal education, much like in school, just wasn't for me. This doesn't mean I don't educate myself along my path, I just choose my own way to go about it.

The key lessons during this time were super important though, with the first lesson in **the value of relationships**. In that role, as a relationship officer, it was my job to manage the relationships with clients within the department. I was in a position where I had to find common ground with people who were far more influential, experienced, and wealthy than I was. I had yet to learn the real value of money at this stage, so I still felt that there was power in a person's monetary value. However, I recall the people I had met, and the joy I felt at times when I was finding myself a part of their worlds. I had clients who had been living in the Middle East and were back home to build a family and life. I had clients who were flipping multimillion-dollar houses as their job, and we would get a chance to see the work they were doing. I had clients who were judges and lawyers, who were from old money and new, who would treat you like a servant and who would treat you as if you were family. I remember once sitting with an elderly couple who had been with the bank for years. They were so kind, and had a son who was a bit older than me, working in the finance sector overseas. To have me managing their account meant the world to them, as I was so much like their son, another young man trying to break into the finance world. They went from being a client to actively wanting to see me succeed. It was at first a strange concept to me that relationships could hold so much value, as I had only ever been part of an admin or service function of a business. But this new value of relationships wouldn't just be apparent in this role, no—it was the beginning of one of my most valuable beliefs in service. The world is a tiny place, and the more you foster prosperous and healthy relationships in your life, especially in the remit of work, the greater the size of your potential success.

The second lesson I learned was that **knowledge is vital to the growth of every person**. There is a belief in my society that the most successful people are those with university degrees. I used to think this was true. Part of me, although I rejected university-level education, felt that I was lacking as a result of not having this degree. However, I have decided that unless you require it for your work, like a doctor or a lawyer requires the formal education of their work, it is actually not as important as we make it out to be. But don't get me wrong—that does not mean I don't believe in expanding our knowledge. There is a huge difference between saying formal education isn't for everyone and we don't need education. I am not saying the latter. Education matters, but it is this concept of knowledge that is imperative for human expansion. It is what we require for the physical growth of our neurological brain, increase in spiritual understanding of life, and change in consciousness. And this can come in many forms. Once you leave high school, some people may find that a formal education is not required for them, and that is OK. But never stop learning in some capacity that is right for you, for an ignorant person is one that is lacking in knowledge.

The last lesson I learned is **the need for joy in the work that we do**. I continued on from my job in the bank and left to work in a travel agency instead. This was a step down in the realms of career path, as I moved away from the prestigious world of private banking to the carpeted shopping mall (literally the shopping mall I worked in had carpeted floors—very dated and tacky) selling retail travel. But for me, it wasn't about trying to prove myself to the world in my career anymore, it was about this new desire to find joy each day I went into that office. I was only young, but I had come to realize that I was so bored of the routine that came with a traditional work life. Waking each day to rush into work in a suit, play businessman all day, then rush home to work out, cook dinner, sleep, and do it all over again. Now this routine is fine, but I suddenly appreciated that it has to be for a reason. And I lacked that reason in banking, as I felt it was an environment that I should have looked at now, rather than as a twenty-one-year-old. So I decided that if I lacked reason for the work I was doing, at least I could find something that would bring me some daily joy. The travel industry offered this to me. I knew I wasn't changing the world, nor did I think that I was going to find my future career path, but what I learned quickly was that it would certainly give me joy each day to be working with a product I cared about and could relate to, and with clients who were easy-going and full of character. But the best part of this change was that it also gave me the space I required to stop and think about my next big adventure.

A DEEPER HUMAN CONNECTION

After working in travel for nine months and learning all about the joy of work, I quickly realized that I had an "itch" to experience work from the soul—something that had real meaning and a positive impact on the world. I may have found some joy in the work I did, but it was not quite fulfilling for my soul, given that I was just booking travel for people. I initially tried looking for other travel jobs that would take me back overseas, thinking they would give me what I needed. I applied for roles with tour companies where I would run tours in countries I hadn't been to. I considered looking at airlines but knew it wouldn't make me happy. I even recall thinking at one point that I would just leave the work I was doing and go mow lawns. Yep, I knew I wanted a change, but I couldn't quite decide what it looked like. I was craving an experience for my soul and I wanted to get my hands dirty, which was translating into some of the craziest ideas I could come up with.

One Sunday, I was at home in my bedroom in our suburban Brisbane town house. I lay on my double bed in the sun coming through the window. My room wasn't large, but it was big enough, with a double bed in the corner of the room and a TV unit at the end of the bed against the opposite wall; my laptop sat on top of it. I had Himalayan prayer flags hung across the top of my window and a side table next to my bed. Incense was burning and I was playing Xavier Rudd on my computer. This was the type of space I would create for myself, especially on days when I was feeling thirsty for something to quench my soul. As it was Sunday, I was beginning to feel the Monday blues early and felt myself hitting a threshold at the thought of going back to yet another pointless week of work.

I used to really struggle with getting up and going to work some days, as I could never understand why we did it. I knew that I needed cash, but for what? This mundane cycle of working to live made me stir-crazy and was part of my constant need for change. I kept trying to find the one ideal thing that would allow me to feel all the different ideas I had in my heart. I thought this would come with a certain job or experience, but no matter what I did, it never lasted very long. This particular day I read something about volunteering overseas. I had already been part of local volunteer programs within Brisbane, including working on weekends with sick children at the Royal Children's Hospital for the past few years, but the idea of doing something similar overseas had not crossed my mind. *What if this is the break I've been dreaming about?* I thought.

I sat up and climbed to the end of my bed for my laptop. I started to Google different volunteer programs and somehow came across an organization called World Youth International (WYI), a not-for-profit, nonreligious, and nongovernmental organization that ran programs in Africa and Asia. Looking at the website, I was drawn to the country of Nepal. I had never heard of it before, but it looked familiar and drew my attention. Before I knew it, I was in, hook, line, and sinker. I decided that I would do a four-month program in Nepal with another ten young Australians. The program was due to begin within the next six months. I had to save money, raise funds for the project, quit my job, and pack up my life in Brisbane. I was so over the routine of my life that something drastic like this felt right. And before I knew it, I had been accepted and was on my way to the Kingdom of Nepal. Little did I know that I would meet people like Dhane who would change my life forever.

Dhane is only a few years older than me, and had the most infectious smile and kindest heart. He was loved by all the team and had been part of World Youth International since it first began work in country back in 2005. On this first project, Dhane was asked by a friend of his, and now a longtime friend of my own, Sanjaya, to come and work. Sanjaya, who was our in-country coordinator, was part of setting up the foundation in Nepal and was integral to ensuring that we found the
projects, funded them, and delivered them, all with a commitment to make sure our Australian volunteers remained safe while they were there.

Dhane, who had lived in Kathmandu since he was fifteen, came from the Mount Everest region of Nepal, high in the mountains. His family was big, but many of his siblings passed away at a young age. He went to school until he was in grade 3, but left after that as they couldn't afford it. By the age of fifteen, Dhane had a sincere desire, an "itch" to go to Kathmandu and find work. He was not formally educated but was seeking work and a better life. He left to Kathmandu, lived on his own, and started working in construction and trekking (like many other men in Nepal). I couldn't imagine what sort of life he experienced being such a young man, working and living on his own in a city that can be difficult for the best of us. But he powered on.

At the age of twenty-one, through Sanjaya, he was introduced to WYI and began work on their projects. His first project was in a remote village in the country. Given most of the population lives in rural communities, this wasn't unusual in the slightest. He was young, and he was eager to be on the project. During his time, he came across a beautiful young lady, Renju, who lived in the community. Well, it must have been fate, as they fell in love by the end of this project. Not only did he get offered some security with work for a few months, but he now met his wife. She, too, was not formally educated, and worked in the fields of the village. Over the following few years, Dhane would work for WYI and continue his trekking, while he and his wife would get married and become pregnant with their little girl, Serina.

So there we were in 2009: Dhane was twenty-five, and I was twenty-one, and this man who we all loved and respected so much was telling me his life story. He was so kind and humble with his words, and his experience astounded me. When he spoke about his little girl, Serina, his eyes would light up, and you could see that he just wanted the world for her. When I asked about his current situation, he explained that he was living in a room near to Thamel with his wife and Serina, who had just started kindergarten in a private school close to their home. I asked if schooling was cheap, to which he said it wasn't. And the challenging part for him was that his work was inconsistent as well! But, he truly believed that because he did not receive an education himself, but could work, that he would do everything possible to ensure that his daughter had the best chance to be educated.

For that moment, I sat there in awe, dumbfounded by his attitude. Here was a man, not that much older than me, with no formal education and no consistent work, but with an attitude and values that were far more commendable than many people that I knew back home. And despite the fact that I do not want to focus on material things, the reality was that this man had next to nothing. But what he did have was his spirit and his values, which were so strong that so many people I knew could have done with chatting to him themselves! I didn't quite know how to respond at first (keep in mind, I was still just twenty-one years old). But his story stuck with me, and I pondered over it for a week. What was I to do with this information? Is there anything I can do with it? Is it actually my business or responsibility to do anything about it? I mean, I was practically a kid, and I didn't even have a job, so what could I really do?

I thought back to the conversation I had at the start of the trip with my team leader, Liss, when she mentioned that she supports some families she met by paying tuition for their children. What if I took the burden of finances away for something that truly mattered to this man? I didn't want a say over anything, or to start dictating conditions, I just wanted to remove a weight from his shoulders given my more ready access to resources. With this thought, I set up some time with Dhane to discuss it. I asked him if he could meet with me in the village after we finished at the work site, so that we could chat about some things. As we were building an additional schoolroom for the local school, our worksite was opposite the classrooms, where we had set up our temporary kitchen and breakout area in one of the free classrooms. We usually met after work to have some chai (local tea) and a snack of some sort. I felt so awkward and uncomfortable at first. What was I doing? Was I being the stereotypical western guy who thinks that he can save the world by throwing some money at a problem? Will he be offended given how hard he works, and that I am trying to show that I can do something that he seems to struggle with so much? As usual, Dhane was kind and happy and made me feel a little calmer once I saw him.

As we started talking, I was feeling a bit overwhelmed by it, and I wasn't even sure what I was going to say. I told him that his story moved me and that I was so proud to meet someone like him who was a similar age to me, had come across so many difficulties, yet had the drive and determination to overcome them. And that this same drive and these same values that he created for himself went far beyond him, influencing the family he was building. It was an amazing thing! I said that, given how I feel and that I have access to certain resources back in Australia, I would like to ask if I could take the responsibility of paying for Serina's school fees. Every year, until she graduates year 12 (and likely into university), I will take on those fees, which will give him the freedom to still work hard to earn his money, but be able to use it for things that his family needs. He looked at me blankly and then smiled. He was overwhelmed. Phew! My worries subsided. I followed up to say that I was not asking for anything more. He is her father; he is responsible for ensuring she works hard for her grades and gets to school, but I will sit quietly in the background and take care of the money. He didn't care for any of that, saying he was more than happy for me to be involved however I like.

It was such a surreal situation. It meant that not only did I get to offer something to a man who I so deeply respected, but I also had the opportunity to create a lifelong relationship with his family. Seven years on, Serina is receiving high grades at school, is superintelligent, and I have such a lovely relationship with all of the family to this day. Every time I go to Nepal, I have the pleasure of going to their home, sitting for dinner, playing some silly games, reading, sharing photos, and continuing our story.

As I said, this story is close to the heart as it tells of a man who comes from a world that was in all ways different to my own, yet held the same values and dreams for his family, as I would for my own. Every day he sought work, for financial freedom and purpose. He woke every day and found a way to be useful and to provide for his family.

The "itch" that I felt in Australia and that led me here, was driven by a need to do more work from my soul, to fill a void, and to attempt to feel more spiritually fulfilled. This experience was beyond anything I expected it to be, and this new connection not only offered me some fundamental life lessons, but it showed me the impact grassroots organizations can have on a community. The trip gave me deeper human connections than I had experienced before; these connections have kept Nepal in my heart until this day.

The first lesson I learned was that *human connections are fundamental to our existence*. As I mentioned, the main part of this experience, outside of living and working in rural communities, was the connection I made to the people around me. It wasn't just Dhane, but the whole group of Australians I was with, along with each family and many of the community members whom I met along the way. Every person had a story to share and a role to play. And in this day and age, where social media and technology connect more of us in the virtual world, we battle with the reality that we are less likely to connect with people in person. We spend so much time consumed by technology and speaking to people on social apps, that we forget the importance of good, old-fashioned, one-on-one conversation. The human connection is so powerful, and as social, energetic creatures, we crave this connection when we don't have it. We may be at work each day and chasing our routine, but when was the last time we really connected with another person, listened to his or her stories, shared your dreams and visions for the future, and found a way to help each other? We cannot underestimate the importance of this for the health of our souls.

My second lesson was understanding that *we are all the same*. This newfound belief was integral to how I perceive the world and for the work I would do in the future. It made me realize that these experiences didn't have to end on the last day of the project. Every day I had an opportunity to connect with someone and create a lasting impact. Whether it was my experience traveling around the globe, or volunteering in Nepal, Australia, or South Africa, what I have learned is that we are all connected and all responsible for our world. For many of us, it is hard enough keeping up with the local issues that go on, let alone the affairs of other countries, but the more we roam this globe and create more technology, the smaller our global community becomes. I truly believe that we are all the same. At the end of the day, once we remove skin color, race, language, culture, religion, environment, and resources, all that really divides us is our perspective. And we can easily change our perspectives if we choose to do so.

THE POWER OF BUSINESS FOR GOOD

Similar to London, after my incredible experience in Nepal I came back to Australia out of money and in desperate need of work. I really didn't think through the aftereffects of such a big shift, and I guess in many ways, I hoped that something would have come after it that I couldn't see at the time. I knew packing up, quitting my job, and moving out of the house I had been living in would create a level of instability later, but I think that is what I was craving. Instead, after that trip, the only thing that was waiting for me was a shift in my deeper perspective of the world and my appreciation for a nice, hot shower. To find work again proved quite difficult. After doing some interim work in recruitment for three months, I decided that I would step back into the last role that brought me joy and start from there, rather than remain miserable hoping for something better. This time, I was in the city dealing with corporate travel. The shine had very quickly worn off from when I had left, and the monotonous city commute (which was no longer on the ferry along the river, as it was in my banking days, but on a miserable train instead) added to the very bland reality I was now experiencing. I couldn't quite adjust myself back into this rat race that I thought we all had to do.

Six months into the job, I was over it. I had the *"itch"* to change jobs and find a reputable brand that would give me more of what I thought I wanted from life—a healthy balance between corporate and philanthropy. But I certainly didn't want to move to the not-for-profit sector, as I needed a decent wage to maintain my lifestyle and to pay off debts that had accrued during my travels, plus I didn't want to be seen as forever jumping from one thing to another. It had to stop. I had to grow up and just be happy to have a job. Surely I couldn't be the only one who is not satisfied. At home one night, I was on Facebook and saw a picture of a woman, Emma, who I knew from my first stint as a travel agent. She was my trainer when I first started in my role, and we stayed in touch. I had a quick look to see where she was in the company now, only to find she had left and was working for one of the leading airline carriers, Virgin Australia. I decided to call on my earliest lesson of courage, and thought I would send her a quick message hello and ask whether she knows of any jobs going. To my surprise, I received a speedy reply to say that she works in staff & duty travel, similar to that of travel agent work but for the airline staff, and was currently hiring. She told me to send her my CV, and I could come for a look. Amazing. I sent the email the next day, and within two weeks, I was in the world of the airline business.

The airline world has built such a reputation for itself, with many people thinking that it must be all glitz and glamour working for one. Well, after seven years in aviation, let me tell you… the benefits undoubtedly give you access to the world, but, my friends, the aviation industry is far from glamorous. What it is, however, is an industry that teaches you how to deliver excellence with as minimal resources as possible. And Virgin Australia, which at the time of joining was "Virgin Blue," did exactly that. I accepted my role in the duty travel team, with a salary that was only $2,000 AUD more than what I was earning in my first job at seventeen—a significant pay cut from my past travel agent roles, where I was making $20,000 more than my Virgin salary. For some reason though, I trusted that it was the right place to be. For the first time, in quite a long time, I felt joy in my daily work again. I was excited to go to work. And I was challenged like never before.

Working for Virgin, I catapulted my career forward. Within six months I was team leader; another twelve months after that I found myself in what they call a "leader" role (which is similar to an assistant manager), and by the time I left, I was marked for a full managerial position, about halfway up the greasy corporate ladder. I met people who have become lifelong friends, traveled the world, was exposed to operations that still to this day fascinate me, and fell even more in love with the idea of flying. Can you believe that those big birds make it in the sky every day? During my time, I also learned about the power of branding, and its impact for guests, for employees, and for the community. Virgin has built an incredibly powerful brand that stands for its people, its customers, and its communities, and in my opinion is the leader in "good business" practices. They are the corporate entrepreneurs, forever shaking up markets and, inevitably, they were part of my inspiration to finally start piecing together how I bridge the gap between business and community.

Over the years, not only did Emma and I work hard to grow our team and develop a department that became loved and respected within the business, but I was lucky enough to be involved in a number of different volunteer programs. This included work with Brisbane Youth Service (BYS) and Virgin Unite, which saw me as part of a six-month advocacy and development program where ten Virgin employees worked alongside ten young people who had been affected by homelessness. We met each week to work on team building and awareness, set up fund-raising events to raise money for BYS programs, create media campaigns around working to end homelessness within Australia, and were part of bigger advocacy events within the community. Being selected within the Australasia region to be part of the annual staff connection trip to South Africa, where ten Virgin employees from around the globe were selected to be part of a weeklong program within a few areas of South Africa, allowed me to engage with and understand the work that Virgin Unite was doing for the global community. This included grassroots community development projects in communities connected with the Virgin Limited Game Reserves, engagement with rural organizations who support those affected by HIV, visiting the flagship Virgin Active in Soweto (the largest township in Africa) which is a shining example of the power of business for "good" based on their strong ties to their community, development of their business around the needs of the people and some incredible success stories for those who came to work for the brand, and spending time at the Branson Centre of Entrepreneurship where they run programs to empower and assist young entrepreneurs in Johannesburg in bringing their ideas to life. Finally, we proposed and kicked off the development of a volunteer program and policy for the Virgin Australia business. While my drive and interest made a lot of this possible, it wouldn't have even been a thought if the business didn't encourage and support it in the first place. It made my time with Virgin hugely interesting, engaging, and beneficial. The more I learned personally and felt engaged, the more I gave back to the business.

This was an integral tool I had to learn in my career. This initial "itch" for more from my work and a better balance was being outdone by being offered a platform where I could really allow this desire to become a reality and excel at what I do, while using this same space to engage with communities and offer support and resources wherever possible. As much as I was able to appease this philanthropic side of me, we worked hard on the corporate front to develop many aspects of the business. I was lucky enough to travel around Australia setting up our duty travel hotels, working with suppliers (who I am fortunate to call my friends still) to develop systems that support our operations, and deal with the everyday dramas that come with running an airline. We were affected by literally everything, which meant I became very good at dealing with last-minute issues and finding the most practical solutions possible. It also meant that I could never really plan, and the more time I spent in aviation, the more I came to understand that.

Over the years, I managed to keep my sights set on the bigger picture with work, as not to misinterpret any "itch" I had as one to move on and take another job. Don't get me wrong, it happened often. Especially during periods of change, where the vision would get a little lost or I would get bored with the work at hand. Thankfully, during these times, Emma, my incredible manager (and one of my best friends now), would talk me off the ledge. We would catch up for morning meetings, usually filled with talking trash and drinking coffee, and she would walk me through why I needed to learn to sit still rather than always fly off—no pun intended. The reason she knew this so well was that she had the same impulses. It was there that we were both busy enough to stay engaged and not need to run elsewhere. In fact, the culture of the business and industry became so consuming that when we did decide to leave, we had no idea what else to do.

But moving jobs was the least of my worries. I look back now and know that the universe had given me the blessings of that work, as it kept me grounded for one of my biggest "itches" yet. It was during my time with Virgin, over the period of about a year, that I came to terms with my sexuality. But the instability that would come from misinterpreting the need to explore my sexuality with something as simple as moving jobs again would have cost me greatly. This is why I trust in my ability to listen to the gut instinct that I keep referring to. That small voice, that "itch" that tells me to bring something into the light to deal with it. It continued to serve as my guiding light in some of the darkest moments of my life.

When I look back at that time at Virgin, I can recognize that my "itch" was more than just a need to have a reputable brand to work for; it was a desire to see how my two ideals of work could come together. Even before my days in banking, I battled with the idea that I had to either be corporate or not-for-profit, a private banker or a social worker, work from the ego or the soul. I believed that these two ideals could never really coexist. But I learned two powerful lessons during this time. The first is one I continue to foster to this day, and it is that **business can be used as a tool for good**. The examples set for me by Virgin, specifically Virgin Unite, paved the way for my entrepreneurial mind to see for myself that one could create businesses that disrupted markets, looked after their people, and used their profits for the betterment of the world. This was as much a lesson as it was a profound insight and something that I continue to work on today, as I look for ways of incorporating these practices into my own business as well as that of others, and to seek out new ways of changing business practices in order to bridge the gap between business and not-for-profit.

The second lesson I learned was thanks to Emma and the opportunities I had across the Virgin Group. I learned a lesson that even transcends working life, and it is that ***perseverance pays off.*** At no point during my time did I feel I was persevering through work that I did not enjoy, or that I was stopping myself from doing something far more significant. Deep down, despite my small *"itches"* along the way, the idea of leaving Virgin never felt right. Even when I felt most disconnected, which was usually related to personal issues rather than work, I would still not want to run like I used to. It was because of this perseverance that I chose to stay put and continue to learn and grow in this space; that I dared to ask for more and take on new responsibilities—to put relationships first and manage them with care. I learned to value my time each day, and ensure that I delivered work on time without impacting my personal life, and to seek joy in all that I do. I found through staying focused in this role that when that "itch" came back in full swing, the opportunities were sitting and waiting for me to pick them up. I didn't have to force them, they just happened, almost as if a reward for my hard work.

I had created habits of running from one dream to another when what I needed most was a chance to stop, reflect, and evolve in other areas of my life, and once I was ready, the universe would place my next adventure in front of me. That is the importance of perseverance. And this lesson has remained valid to me, even until today.

COMING OUT

If you ask many people within the LGBT+ community, you will find that they have their "coming-out" story. This is a time of darkness, lies, confusion, anger, hurt, disappointment, betrayal, and rejection. Especially for those generations before ours. It is a time where, for some, their life is in question, as this type of identity and "choice," as some people falsely love to believe, is not accepted by society. It is a time where we have thousands of different stories, which ultimately affect not only the individual but also the community at large.

As I mentioned, a part of me always felt like I was missing something in my life, and as you will learn, I did everything I could to find out who I was. I undertook this search for my authentic self through the work I did, the people I spent time with, the books I read, and the views I held for the world. Even to this day, it remains a journey of discovery, as I truly believe life should. There is no endgame, just a constant evolution of self and soul.

It was around the age of twenty-three, when I was in a place of dissonance between how I felt inside versus how people perceived me, that I could no longer ignore. To the world around me, I was a happy and charismatic man. The ladies seemed to have eyes for me, I had a rational view of the world, and I was close to my family. I was always progressing in my career and I loved to travel. I loved having beers at the pub with my brothers, going to the beach, and watching the footy. I did have a spiritual side to me and loved charity, but I thought that I was just lucky to see the needs of the world and want to help. To most people, I was what could be perceived as a typical heterosexual male. But despite all of this, inside I was battling with something different. I would meet these girls, and they would seem amazing, but I could never see a future with them. Sex was always okay but I didn't get excited about sex like other male friends of mine did. They would all be so keen to go out on a Saturday night and meet some "birds" (Australian slang for women), but I would always feel like it was such hard work. I assumed this was a result of being a little more emotionally in tune with myself, but as time went on, the feeling grew stronger. And after spending my formative years forcing myself, subconsciously, into this person I believed I was, or that I should be, something cracked. It was like the role had expired and I felt like I could no longer put on a charade. With hindsight, after a good number of years understanding who I am and going through my discovery even while writing this book, I am still now remembering different things from my past that I chose to ignore, or deluded myself into believing. It is a shame to think that through expectations set by society, and our family and friends, we prefer to ignore certain feelings and focus on being what we expect we are "meant" to be, rather than what we honestly feel we should be.

If I think back to my younger self, I can now start to reflect and recall different thoughts, feelings, and emotions that I had which I couldn't place and chose to ignore. I always remember feeling different as a child, but given my existing story of an acute skin condition, it didn't take me long to immediately identify with that as to why I was feeling a certain way. So far, my earliest recollection of these different feelings comes from when I was nine years of age. It was 1997, I was in grade 4, and the pop group, Hanson, had just launched into our worlds. I remember seeing one of the brothers—Taylor, I think it was—and something reacted inside of me. It was strange; it was this feeling that I couldn't place. It was a sense of attraction, but not in the same way I had felt before, and not for a guy. I assumed I was a little starstruck or something, so ignored it at the time, but have clear memories of this feeling. Other examples of these feelings came later in life when watching shows like *Queer as Folk* when I was fifteen, and being intrigued by it, not because of the gay porn, but because it was this life I had never even comprehended before now. Despite at the time finding myself turned on, I told myself that it was normal as I was fifteen and figuring life out. Obviously, a legit reason that I used to convince myself. Or the time when I was seventeen and had an encounter with a male friend when we were drunk, which was as innocent as me, consciously in a drunken state, moving my hand under a blanket and brushing past his crotch. He knew he was gay, although I don't think he had "come out," and so he suggested we take this elsewhere, to which I freaked out and retreated immediately. Only to spend the next week self-loathing and telling myself that it was another "normal experience" that we have to go through. All the way to watching porn with two men and a woman, and being more interested in the men. Again, delusion and conditioning said that it was OK and to ignore it.

Away from the emotional feelings toward men, there were experiences around the way in which I identified with myself, which I can now see as the world trying to show me my authentic self. I recall when I was eleven years of age and Mum had just dropped me off to school. As I walked in, my mum called out to me and told me to change the way I was walking. She said, "Don't walk like that, Luke, clench your fists some more and don't let your hands hang by your side." I had no idea where it came from, and even now, I am sure my mother would be mortified to hear that she once said it. Maybe she didn't mean it in a negative way, or maybe she did. But I am sure at that point in her own life, she acknowledged that her son was walking in a way that maybe triggered particular thoughts, fears, or identities for her. Still to this day, as the person receiving the feedback, I can recall the moment, the feeling, the memory, so explicitly. It was as if it had just happened. I also remember that from this defining moment onward, I chose always to be super aware of how people perceived me in public during my formative years. How I was acting, how I spoke, how I interacted with people was always consciously in my mind, especially in school.

When I was in high school, and I was around thirteen or fourteen, I was right into my performing arts and used to love coming home and putting on the soundtrack to *Moulin Rouge*, for instance, to dance around the house as if I was performing for a crowd. My imagination would go wild, and I would perform my heart out. At the same time, I recall going to school and being bullied by other guys as I would spend most of my time either with girls or in the performing arts community. Like everyone in high school, I spent my time trying to find the crowd of people that best suited me. My peers in the performing arts community all experienced, in one way or another, the same prejudice, which I think only brought us closer. It seems within our school system, at least when I was there, people ridiculed the creative types as they didn't meet the sporting image of "cool" that everyone thinks they should aspire to. One guy, in particular, was going to "bash me" as I was "a fucking homo"—I had never done anything to him, it was just through his perception of me that he decided I should be hurt. Thankfully, no physical fight took place, but it was emotional turmoil at that age. I had quite a good reputation with girls, so they all just said it was because he was jealous, but to me, I was being bullied and set upon for something I felt didn't exist and could not see. Even to this day, I can't tell you how much I played into the stereotype of being a "ladies' man," but my capacity to connect with the female population impacted my world in high school, especially to young, pubescent men.

I came across the same level of bullying at only one point in Brisbane, in grade 11, to the extent where I wanted to leave school and just work instead. Thankfully, I was convinced otherwise and stuck to it. Only to find that I discovered my strength in grade 12 and called the bullies out for the weak people they were. I recall the day I was walking to the canteen from our usual lunchtime hangout under a covered pergola seating area between blocks C and D. I walked past a group of guys, who every second or third day, depending on what ridiculous mood they were in, would yell out names or torments at me. I usually ignored it while my face flushed and I felt a little more anger and resentment build inside. If I was walking with a female friend, she would sometimes yell back at the guys and tell me to ignore them, but I usually just pretended it didn't happen or that they were yelling at someone else. But this day, I decided I'd had enough and there was no way for me to pretend it wasn't for me. So, after they yelled some ridiculous statement at me, usually about the fact that I was a "poof," I turned around and retaliated. I responded not with anger, but with an observation that they might think I was gay, but I wasn't the one who was obsessing over another man every day. I shamed them publicly at a pitch that ensured all of my peers heard. This didn't go down well. Everyone who heard me burst out laughing and their embarrassment was so sweet, even though I know it wasn't kind. But in that moment, I won back my own power and place and stopped any name-calling in the future. I think the hilarious part about high school drama is when those same guys would try and befriend me in my twenties. I mean, I would never continue to judge them for their mistakes, but really? Come on, guys.

Lastly, I recall when I was around seventeen and had a spiritual reading. I hadn't had one on my own before and I was a little nervous about what to expect. As with all things in life, I had already set expectations for what I wanted her to tell me when I went. I was with Karley at the time, and so I was hoping she would tell me that the love I felt for her was right and that I would spend the rest of my life with her. Basically, I had this idea that the psychic would simply validate all of my preconceived ideas that I had created about my reality and how it *should* be.

It was around 7:00 in the evening and I remember driving up to the psychic's house in my small, yellow Mitsubishi Lancer named "Gaz"—aka, Gary good car. Her house was on a hill and I recall sitting in my car for a bit before I went in, unsure about what to expect. She was a friend of my mum's whom she had only met recently, and so I felt okay going in because she knew my family, but it was a strange concept for me. We sat down, and she used tarot cards to do my reading, along with some form of jewelry that I had. At the time, because I had a clear idea what I *wanted* to be told, I was half listening and just trying to find any words she said that would validate what was in my mind. If you believe in readings, you know this is a no-no.

As the reading went on, she told me a range of information like the different countries I would live in and visit throughout my life, including Abu Dhabi, which she struggled to pronounce clearly. She told me that it started with "A," that it was an island and was in the middle of the world. She said I would be working in a field where I would be dealing with people in all different time zones. But one thing she did say, which to a seventeen-year-old who was "straight," only made sense to validate my repression of any "gay" feelings, was that in my life I would have to find the right balance between my masculine and feminine sides. I would see that I need to keep my femininity in check, she said. She also went on to say that I could have had this life as a woman, but I have been sent here as a man, as I have work to do and wouldn't have had the same platform as a woman in this day and age. To me as a seventeen-year-old, I thought, great—this answers why I am straight but have these crazy little moments along the way. It is all about growing up. To me as a thirty-year-old, I can see that it means something much more significant than anything I could have understood at that time.

Now, this isn't to say that these experiences are what define "gay people." No, this is to say that my world was showing me signs, but through a world of conditioning, whether conscious or subconscious, with intention or without, from my perception or that of those around me, I was choosing to avoid or ignore them. So at the age of twenty-three, when I didn't have my thirty-year-old self to speak to, these memories were so profoundly dismissed that it came as a shock to me that I was so lost in my relationships, and had this thought that maybe I hadn't explored my sexuality enough. I mean, so far, I had questioned everything around me, including my own spiritual beliefs, but the thought of challenging my sexuality seemed crazy!

I tried so hard up until this point to tap into my "crazy twenty-something-year-old," who went out and met girls and shagged around. No matter how much I tried to tap into that feeling or that way of thinking, I just couldn't quite get there. It was like I was missing something. "Maybe I am just not that type of guy," I used to think. I grew up with my mum and sister for most of my life, so maybe I just have a lot of respect for women. Surely I can't follow in the footsteps of my brothers (who, their younger selves will love me saying, ensured they had their fair share of women while growing up).

In addition to feeling that something was missing, I never quite felt comfortable in my skin, despite continually working to develop my opportunities, knowledge, ambitions, and personal brand. I put myself out to volunteer, grow my knowledge through hundreds of different social, political, and personal development books, traveled the world to expand my mind and see what was on offer. Still, after all this, when it came to relationships, I just didn't feel right. What could it be? Why is it we are so defined by our societal expectations of sexuality, by this heteronormativity that so many of us are born into, that we refuse to accept who we truly are? Why is it that so many men and women grow up trying to fit into a box, spending their days so miserable and depressed from the confines of these expectations, until one day they break and can no longer exist in that way? For many, they find love in the opposite sex and force themselves to change their ways, while for many others, they will hold the feeling so tight that it will leak into other forms in their life, like poison in a river. It breaks my heart. But why did I spend so many years in this same category? And how did I manage to get myself out?

I will take you through my experiences now, the whole package, including my "coming-out" relationship, which I believe is an integral part of the experience.

The Shift of Thought
It was 31 December, 2011, and my brothers, some friends of ours, and I decided last minute to head out for New Year's Eve antics at a local hotel in Brisbane, Australia. New Year's in Australia occurs during the peak of summertime, so it's hot outside, even at night. Luckily, we were inside a large, modern bar in what was once a fairly traditional Australian pub close to the river. The evening was quiet at the beginning, but as the night played out and the alcohol kicked in, the dance floor lit up and gradually filled with people. After drinking a few beers myself, I was playing up to my mischievous nature of my age. I think at one point I had kissed a handful of different girls on and around the dance floor, and I had no cares in the world. Midnight went as quickly as it came, and we all celebrated the New Year. We continued to party on after, but decided it was enough for the night. As the evening came to an end, an old flame found me at the bar. We had met a year or two before when we were working at the Children's Hospital. She was a lovely and kind woman, a few years older than I, and we seemed to always get along fairly well. It was one of those relationships where we would try and get it off the ground, but for some reason it would stall every time. But we continued to bump into each other along the way. As we spoke, she told me that she had her car with her and offered to take me home. I knew what that might mean, and questioned whether I was up for it. Naturally, as the taxi queues grew in length and the drunk Luke decided he was to keep charging on with his silly behavior, I agreed, and we left for home. That night she stayed. I was drunk, and I am sure quite average when it came to sex, but it was fun. The next morning she woke and had to do the walk of shame past the living room where my brothers, sister, brother-in-law, and anyone else that could be in the house, happened to be sitting. Poor girl! Everyone was quiet and decided to cheer on after she left. You know, the usual gratification of a "job well

done." For a moment, I felt good about myself. I was doing what I had set out to do. I am that "man," but deep down it still felt unfulfilling.

Days passed, and I was not interested in seeing her again. In fact, something was agitating me about the whole situation. I was capable of having these relationships, and I enjoyed the sex for what it was. I mean it wasn't mind-blowing, but it was enjoyable. I was good at it, I think. But it lacked in something. Maybe this is just what it is like when you are finding yourself in your twenties.

A few weeks later I was at home in bed on a Sunday night. I was lying there, reflecting and writing in my journal. This was a normal practice for me, especially on a Sunday night. It was that moment when you go to bed, prepare for the week ahead and for the potential of "Monday blues" that awaits you. But for some reason that week, something inside of me felt more perplexed than normal. It was more than just a feeling of hating my job, dreading the tasks of the coming week, or feeling just a bit flat after a weekend of likely drinking and/or partying. It was a feeling of knowing that I was not being honest with myself. Imagine a dam filled with water, that has been slowly filling day after day. The dam looks strong from afar, but a crack has begun to form along the front of the structure. This crack happened when small chips began to break away—a series of bad relationships, a lackluster one-night stand, people talking about their exciting sex lives, judgment from others about your own sexuality and worth. All of these small digs, mishaps, or breakdowns contributed to the crack in the dam. As I was pondering this feeling that I couldn't shake, not knowing that this dam was inside, something I had chosen to ignore for years and that played quietly in the back of my mind came rolling like thunder across the plains. Despite now looking back and knowing the truth, at the time it was like an epiphany to my conditioned and sheltered mind.

"What if I'm gay?"

And just like that, it was as if the dam walls broke and the water came rushing out. I didn't know how to hide the thought any longer. The moment I allowed myself to say it, it was like I couldn't turn back. What if, after all these years, the final piece of missing information in creating the whole me, is that I am identifying with the wrong sexuality? All of a sudden, it was like I handed myself over to the vulnerability of that reality and my mind became inundated with different memories, thoughts, and ideas that I had labeled as "something else" over the years. Similar to the examples of Hanson, *Queer as Folk*, and the experience with my high school friend, I recalled memories of simple things like watching porn with both men and women and being interested more in the men, encounters I'd had with male friends when I lived overseas that I did my best to avoid, even old feelings of being attracted to particular males, but believing that it was just an attraction of wanting to be *like* them, rather than be *with* them. These all seemed to make more sense in the context of owning that I was, and dare I say it, gay.

For so many guys, this moment of coming out is a range of things. It can be an oppressed feeling for years or a natural process that they knew from birth. But, ultimately, it is a highly personal process filled with fear, sadness, anxiety, excitement, hope. The list goes on. For me, it was a time when even the faint thought of the idea that I was gay meant I not only questioned who I would take to bed with me, but who I would then share my life with, and in turn the lives of my family. Until now, I was super close to my family. We shared a bond that I was grateful for every day. After all of the challenges we have shared together in life, the one thing we did was come closer together. It created a unit that was unbreakable up until now. However, even at the very thought of this, my mind wandered to the fact that I could be stepping into a reality that could not only break me but could break my family.

My New Daily Lessons and Struggles
I guess once I broke it to myself that I was likely "barking up the wrong tree" when it came to my love life, things became a slow and ever-changing landscape. The first stage was obviously further and full denial. I would find myself going to bed each night, a time when I would normally immerse myself into my dreams before sleeping; where I would read books, write about my future, imagine a day when I felt fully alive. And, yet, instead of all of this, I would be lying there thinking about my possible new reality. "If I am gay, what do I even do with it? Where do I start? Do I just start talking to guys? Gross. I cannot believe that I am even considering this? Maybe porn will do. I am sure it is just a phase. I know plenty of straight guys who have threesomes with both men and women. It is normal. I am overreacting."

This stream of dialogue would go on, while at the same time the usual inquisitive me would start searching the internet for something more enticing than my thoughts. It began with porn. Obviously. I had seen some over the years, and it felt safe. It didn't mean I was gay; it just implied I could watch this and no one would know. It is my own life after all. But after a while, the interest pushes you further. For many people who went through this same "coming out" in previous years, this would have been a time of deep struggle and confusion as well. The difference being, they had to find somewhere to let that out in the public domain. As a member of generation Y, I had other options—namely, I could go into the land of the world wide web.

One night I was lying in bed, thinking back on the day. I recalled I was at a friend's desk at work, and they were laughing about a gay friend of theirs who had been using this mobile app to chat and meet guys. I had no idea these even existed at that point. I wasn't quite up with technology when it came to meeting people. I recall her telling me the name—Grindr. (I am sure many of you who are gay are giggling at this point.) Little did I know that this app would be the start of my new sex life, sexuality, and a world of situations and people I had never even imagined I would meet.

For those that don't know, Grindr is a mobile app for gay men to chat and meet. I thought I would download it, as curiosity would make my head spin, and see what it was all about. I remember going on there for the first time. All of these photos of faces and torsos popped up, anonymous by name, but describing themselves with age and sexual preference. I was petrified and left mine incognito, as I worried that I would come across someone I knew. I did work in aviation after all, which happened to have a large gay community. I began chatting with people. They were always interested to know who you were, but I could only give away so much information. The first time I was talking with some guys, and they would just send me dick pics or ask what my sexual preferences are, or see if I was "looking," I had no idea what was going on. So for the first few weeks, I spent most of my time chatting with guys, working myself up to the point of being all hot and bothered, and then I would freak out and close the app.

The First Line Was Crossed

It was a few weeks in, and I was starting to enjoy chatting with different people. In fact, I had started talking to a variety of guys more regularly. I started to become comfortable sharing my story of realizing I was gay, but I still didn't know what to do about it.

I learned this wasn't something new, and they were very kind with their words and time. I found some comfort in these conversations and in their anonymity. One night, I came home from a night out with friends after a few beers. I was relaxed and comfortable and slid into bed relatively early for a Friday night. I opened the app and started talking with this guy who I had been chatting with for a while at that point. He was lovely, born in New Zealand, and only lived around the corner from me. We started talking as usual, but this time he was home alone and asked if I wanted to meet in person. My heart started racing, but the beers were still in effect. I said that it was late, trying to find a way to avoid it. He asked me again, and said it was good to meet in person to get over that hurdle. I panicked inside, but something told me to go and at least say hi. I think between the fear of actualizing the situation which held me back, and the deep desire to simply find peace and happiness in who I was discovering, I decided to take the risk and head over to his house. When I walked in I would have been acting like such a weirdo! I remember thinking I was in some parallel universe. To put it in perspective, I was a stranger walking into another stranger's house late at night, irrelevant of our sexuality. So yeah, I probably should've been cautious.

As it turned out, he was lovely. Such a kind guy. Same age as me, soft in his word, handsome, and fit. And he had just had a shower and had this particular scent on him that reminded me of hemp oil or something from the body shop. Somehow it made me feel calm as it was a familiar smell. We chatted for a while, him asking me about my situation of coming out and me, again, likely acting like some weirdo in response. Ugh. I mean, it is just such an awkward time! Eventually, he said he was watching a movie in his room and asked if I would like to join. I may have been coming out, but I was not stupid. At this point, a "Netflix and Chill" didn't exist, but I knew what was going on.

Lying on his bed, I was so aware of everything that was happening. My heart was racing, and I worried that someone would come in. Within about five to ten minutes, his foot began rubbing mine. My heart beat faster. I rubbed back. My breathing increased, and I started questioning everything. Before you knew it, we moved in, rolled over, and began to make out. At this stage, I was freaking out in my mind. It was this strange, out-of-body experience where I was so aware of what was happening and enjoying it mixed with old prejudices that this was "wrong" and that it shouldn't be happening. I felt that I had crossed a line and wouldn't be able to turn back. But, as the moment went on, I started to realize that actually he was a good kisser, and this situation was not as scary as I'd thought. We made out some more, and one thing led to another. He started making his way elsewhere on my body, and I let it happen. By that point I thought, *fuck it. I can forget it ever happened if it isn't right. This moment is just how you experience life.*

After I finished, it was like this release from my body. Not just physically, but emotionally. I felt liberated and freed from the unknown. I knew it was only the beginning, but so much of my fear was a realization that I was gay and that I had never really been with a guy before. I couldn't understand how I could think I was gay without ever having been with someone of the same sex. Now that it had happened, it was a relief in so many ways. I sat up afterward, slightly freaked out once the sexual bliss had subsided, and immediately thought, *I need to get out of here!*

I jumped up and said I had better leave. He knew that would be the case and accepted, asking if we could catch up again. At that point, I couldn't even think straight, no pun intended, let alone agree to see him again.

By the time I got home, showered, and hopped into bed, I had calmed down and started to feel good. In fact, I felt relieved, and I felt better about everything. The reality of accepting that I was now being physically intimate with other men was still unresolved for me as it was still so new, and as I said, the idea was riddled with prejudice built up by my own conditioning—but the sexual interaction felt more full, and fulfilling, than my experiences with women. I had been missing something, and the energy of being with a man felt so much more in tune with what I had been seeking. There was this satisfaction, this exchange of energy that had taken place which I always felt I had been missing, and it was what I would expect after sex. It was a feeling of being satisfied but also wanting more. For the first time, I had sex and I was thirsty for more, rather than relieved that it was over. Little did I know, this was the beginning of a very long road of learning and discovery—which was coupled with a very dark period of my life when I had to find myself again in a world of uncertainty, validation, expectations, and love.

Discovery Phase: The good, bad, and downright stupid
I met with my kiwi neighbor a few weeks later. After we had first met, I made a promise to myself that I wouldn't meet another guy again for a while, as I needed to get my head around the whole thing first. That empty promise lasted a week or two, and I was back at it. This time, things were not quite as awkward, but I still had my moments. Sexually I was more interested in trying different things, but I'm sure I wasn't very great at them. But the main awkwardness came when I would speak about normal life—who you are, what you do, who you live with. For a man who was not out about his sexuality, it felt like a minefield littered with potential bombs waiting to go off and blow my cover.

As time started to tick over, I found out a lot about different people on this app. Some guys were in the same position as me. Others were nowhere near coming out, and were instead indulging in a very dark secret, sometimes even behind a current hetero lover's back. And then there were those who were fully living their authentic selves and just trying to meet guys this way. I chatted with lots of guys. I learned all about how people judge you based on your photo and preferences (there's not a great deal of simply talking with anyone on Grindr) and how most of the people, irrelevant of whether they say something about being there just to "chat," are looking for sex. For me, this wasn't a bother, as I figured that it was the purpose of the app given some of the crazies I would come across, but for many others, I know this can be tiring.

At the start, I wouldn't just meet up with randoms; I had to vet them first. Meet in person, chat for a while, make sure I feel comfortable with them, and after that we could hook up. It was a weird and wonderful world when I first started learning all about what it means to be gay—well, at least when it comes to sex. It wasn't long before I began to have sex. The thrill of it all was sparking a part of my brain that had felt so dried up and empty. I was finally getting all the elements I thought I was missing. The chemistry I found in being with men was what made my new reality sink in. It wasn't what the gay community offered (at that point I didn't even know it existed), it wasn't having some deep and meaningful conversation with these people—it was just the sexual chemistry and emotional response I was having to it. There was something about the power and strength of a man that satisfied me sexually. The smell, the sounds, the interaction. It was not that I was being dominated by them, but even lying with a man; his needs felt so different than those of a woman. This is where my emotional response changed as well. I felt less pressure from men to meet an expectation than I had felt from women (which is not a poor reflection on women, just my preconceived ideas conditioned over time). To be with a man felt exciting; it felt fulfilling and, for the first time in my life, it felt natural.

After a while, I had been with a few different guys, found myself in some strange and hilarious situations late at night, and noticed that I had started to create a second life for myself. I was living what my family and friends knew and saw, which at this stage was for most of my time. But I had this other life ticking over, that I was slowly fostering and giving energy. This different life would find me in situations that no one else knew. I would be staying at a boy's house, even though I told those around me it was some girl I was seeing. I was sneaking out late at night to meet up with a new hot boy I had found online. I would ignore every conversation with friends that came up about sex or relationships. I was becoming infatuated—almost obsessed with guys. This obsession started to hold some power over me. It was beginning to control my thoughts and my actions. And worst of all, I was beginning these weird relationships built solely on sex, with no real depth or value to them, in order to feel like I was validated or accepted. I didn't want just to have sex; I needed to see that I could also be "wanted" in return. It was as if my emotional connection with men was understood, but I wasn't getting the acceptance I felt I required. But was it required from them, or was this becoming my reality as I had not properly accepted myself at this stage?

Once the thrill of the mobile app started to wear down, I found I had other urges and that I was feeding this "animal" of mine way more than what was healthy. I believe we all have our own sexual "animals" that we need to choose to support. We can feed it often and in large portions, to which it will continue to expect that in the future, or we could decide to feed it in small, healthier amounts. The choice is ours. I was finding that meeting men one-on-one was fun, interesting, and grew my own network of people in my community. However, it was also filled with personal connections, emotions, and the potential for me to be "outed" if I ever met the wrong person. Because I had kept my sexuality at bay for so long, I felt like a teenager discovering sex for the first time. I didn't realize I had all these sexual fantasies and ideas I wanted to explore. My animal was out of control, starving, and always looking for food. I was in such an anonymous phase of life, a big part of me felt the desire to explore these urges. But how? Where would I go to explore something beyond one-on-one sex with a stranger?

The "itch" for more came one night after I left drinks with friends in the Valley. We had been out at a Japanese gyoza place and had a delightful evening. I had been battling the crazies in my head and telling myself that I would give everything a bit of a break, as I felt off center. I also thought that if this is all being "gay" means—going on these silly apps and not getting enough sleep—then I would rather pass on that. I left dinner boozed up and feeling good with life. I was in the Valley on a Friday night on my own and had to make my way home. I walked past a club that I had never seen before. It took my interest immediately, and I couldn't figure out why. I crossed the road, as not to be seen in front of it, and Googled the name (the joys of Gen Y world). It was a gay "cruise club." What the hell is a cruise club? From what I could see it said that it's a place where gay men go to have sex. These existed outside of porn? My heart started racing, and the animal inside was *hungry* all of a sudden. I went to walk away, but I was boozed and thought *you only live once*—so I walked over.

It's funny that in these situations, it feels like your mind goes blank, your ears ring, and your adrenaline is pumping, so much so that you don't even really know what you are doing. All of your senses become heightened! I walked up to the club and paid at the door, and a kind, bald, quite tall, and overtly sexual man was there to greet me and take my money. He gave me a look that felt like he was saying, "I know your secret." I walked in, and the place was dark but busy. Men were walking around, purposefully but with no real endgame. Some men were at the bar chatting, and the TVs played quite explicit gay porn. I bypassed any of the social interactions and made my way through the maze of rooms—a dungeon, a room with a sling hanging from the ceiling, a million different places to hook up. It was one big sex club. I didn't quite know what to do, so I found a space in a room with seating and an enormous screen on which porn was playing. I sat there, nervous, watching those around me move between rooms, cruise one another, and hook up. The establishment was like nothing I had experienced. The feeling of being there was so foreign to me, but it was so sexual and comforting. It was a place where you could anonymously get those deep sexual dreams out of your body, where no one will ask any questions.

Once I began to relax in the space, I started to get involved in a few group activities, mainly finding myself just standing there, while everyone else did the work. Men began to come up and start grabbing my body. It began with one or two men, which was hot. It was like an out-of-body experience. To start with, I felt very turned on, but I also felt dirty and this feeling progressively got worse. Why was I craving this type of physical and sexual attention all of a sudden? What had I missed out on before, that I believed this needs to be the way in which I get satisfied? Why weren't my previous one-on-one hookups enough, that I needed this? Before I knew it, a few more joined the group. I didn't realize that some people are shy, but once something kicks off, everyone wants in. Before you know it, my pants were down, my shirt was lifted up, and I couldn't even tell you how many different men were grabbing, kissing, and touching my body. It was completely overwhelming. I nearly fell backward, but lo and behold someone was there to catch me. It suddenly got intense, not that anything had changed, but I freaked out. All of a sudden, I started pushing people off me, trying to untangle myself. What was I doing there? Is this what I wanted? I made my way out of the group of what felt like vultures, got myself together, and made my way to the door. I busted out of that building, scurried down the walkway, made sure no one saw me, and quickly walked to the bar where my brother was working. I felt vulnerable, dirty, confused, dark, and upset. What was I doing with my world?

Like all of these experiences, it didn't take long until the self-loathing disappeared and the "animal" came to life again. This sexual "animal" wanted to be satisfied so often; I didn't know how to tame him. The only way I knew, was to keep doing what I was doing—sexually explore what felt like most of Brisbane! I had plenty of positive experiences though, meeting guys who I befriended, started to chat with, and with whom I would often hang out. I was beginning to understand this new world I was entering. Some of the experiences were even quite fun. They were usually just with other guys like myself, looking for some excitement. At the same time, I came across some strange ones too. There was probably a handful of times, out of—dare I say it—a considerable amount of men, who made me feel unsafe, unsure, or just a little bit on edge. I had one experience with a guy where halfway through hooking up, I simply got up and left, as I didn't feel safe all of a sudden. I had another time where this guy was a bit older, and after a quite intense session, he started examining my hands, feet, and body, telling me just how beautiful I was. Not in a "Thanks, you're cute too" way, either. It was more of a, "If I don't leave now, I feel like I may be skinned and worn for the evening" kind of way.

One night, after I got home from being out with friends (are you sensing a theme here?) I was tired and ready for bed—but, of course, I got online and started chatting. This guy and his boyfriend were looking for some fun, and weren't too far away. For some reason, the "animal" came to life, despite my body and soul being exhausted, and I found myself driving over to their house. As I arrived, this tall, average-looking guy whom I had been chatting with online met me out front. It was dark, so I couldn't quite see him clearly, but he seemed like his picture. From what I could tell, he was either drunk or high, but he wasn't too bad. The house was big. Again, it was dark, but it was an old two-story building in the outer suburbs. It seemed weird that a guy his age would live in a house like this. But I was too tired to ask questions. We walked inside, and immediately I wanted to leave. The place was perfectly clean and modern, but stepping inside felt like entering an old haunted house. We walked in, went upstairs, and he was chatting about something. I was looking around thinking, *you two can't own this house*—not only was it huge, but the rooms were filled with the kind of stuffy, oversized furniture favored by an older generation. It was not to the tastes of two young gay men in Brisbane. I was right. By the time we got to the top of the stairs and walked to his room, someone who seemed to be his dad or grandpa—an elderly man—came out of the room opposite and started yelling something at us, "This house isn't for your damn sex parties."

I must have looked like a deer in headlights. The guy laughed, told him to shut up and continued into his room, where his boyfriend was on the bed smoking a joint and laughing. All of a sudden, this "hot" idea of going to their house turned vile, and it was as if every alarm bell possible went off inside me. I stopped at their door, shook my head and said, "Yep, I won't be staying." With that I turned, went past the crazy old man again, ran down the stairs and out the door to my car, and with one hell of a spin drove it like a madman down the street and immediately back home. I felt foul. That entire situation, especially being exposed to that elderly gentleman and the lack of respect the guys showed him, completely went against my most fundamental values. It was a horrible experience. As soon as I was home, the self-loathing and immediate regret kicked in.

"What the fuck had I got myself into? Who the hell am I becoming? This reality is so far from who I am authentically. Why do I keep going to get myself into these gross situations? Never again. Never. Ever. Again."

The "Coming-out" Relationship

After a few months of this type of crazy behavior, I had my fair share of chaos, sleepless nights, weird and unusual encounters, and a plethora of new experiences under my belt. It was around maybe the six-month mark when I met a guy online who said he was also a physio. Amazing. *He must have nice hands,* I thought. He invited me to his house for some fun, but said it would be in his practice room as his housemate might come home in between. It was slightly unusual, but I went with it. As I arrived and met him, he had such a kind face. I felt instantly comfortable with him. We went into his room and started chatting. One thing led to another and we began hooking up. And as expected, halfway through, his housemate came home. The place was small so you couldn't really continue to do anything without disturbing everyone else. We quietly laughed and got dressed. He asked if I would like an adjustment or a checkup, to which I thought *Why not?* I liked this guy. There was something about him that felt comforting, especially after such a turbulent six months. We met up again in the following weeks and I developed feelings for him, which led us into a relationship. He was a nice guy, despite all of his hang-ups (as we all have). At the time, outside of some small but strange behaviors I picked up on, I accepted him for who he was. He gave me what I felt I needed during this period of my life, and was a kind and loving person at heart. I learned more about me in this relationship and began to find my way in this new world, with a partner by my side. As expected, I was not in the best place emotionally at the time, feeling disconnected from my family and friends, lost with who I was identifying with and, now, trying to forge a relationship with another person when I could barely form one with myself.

I remember back to this relationship, feeling almost like a schoolboy again. That young, puppy love emotion, where you get so excited to receive a message or hang out with them. I recall leaving work at lunchtime to rush over to his place for some midday fun so that I could see him. It was sweet. But, it was also now starting to impede on my family and friends. I began introducing him to the people I love as a new "friend." I had initially met him getting some physiotherapy done, so I think I just used this as how we knew each other. He would start coming to my house, and we would sit in the car for hours just chatting, with a sneaky kiss here and there. I would be late to dinner with friends, as I would go to his place beforehand, and I had to start explaining why I suddenly had this new best friend, despite the behavior being so inconsistent to anything those around me knew before (including myself).

As time went on, things became more intense. I found myself trying to create certain aspects of a relationship that I wanted in a boyfriend, but I was having difficulty doing so as the basis of this relationship was effectively a lie. It was small things like going to his house, cooking dinner, and spending the night; or going to the movies together; or hanging out on the weekend; or even having him come to my house to spend time with me, but only when my family was away. I was trying to create these elements of our relationship, but they were flawed. How could I foster a healthy relationship when we were lying to the world about it? It didn't feel right, and was part of why the relationship began to fracture.

The Dark Comes to Light

After nine months of coming to terms with this new reality; of pushing myself into the unknown that broke all that I knew, and starting a life that I wasn't even ready to accept, I couldn't hide it any longer. Every moment I looked at my family, I felt terrible for not being honest. Every time I looked at myself, I knew I was not truthful to my heart. Every time I sat with my dreams of the future—imagining me in a healthy, loving relationship with a handsome and kind man who both my family and I loved—I knew I was sitting in a place where the life I lived now and the dreams I had for the future did not match. The reality is that I started to shift into an internal world of darkness. I didn't feel even semi-complete like I had before. I just felt out of sync. And it hurt. I felt like the light that I'd once felt inside of me was dim. I felt like every day I had to keep up with my own lies in order to save face with those around me and ensure that my story always checked out. I felt as if I was stepping further and further away from who I was and who I thought I should be. I felt like a liar. And never in my life had I seen myself as a liar, especially not to my loved ones. But most of all, I felt inauthentic. I felt like I was in a constant state of being out of body and on edge.

Luckily for me, the more that time went on, the more difficult it was to hide how I was feeling. And my family, who knew me better than anyone else, could see that something wasn't right. They would try and ask me if I was okay, but I would avoid any discussions so as to not get upset and release these bottled-up emotions that lay dormant beneath the surface. I felt lost, ashamed, vulnerable, scared, and cornered more than ever before. I would find myself hiding from family when they came over, avoiding subjects that may raise questions about the cover I had created. I would wake up each morning with two agendas for the day and a sick feeling in the pit of my stomach that was a mix of anxiety and frustration. For the first time in my life, I couldn't see what the future would look like. I couldn't see my dreams and the vision I had for the life I wanted to live. All my life I prided myself on my ability to have a clear vision of my future, even if it wasn't what I thought would happen, but at this stage, I could barely see what the next day would look like. My self-esteem was low, my value was low, and I believed that I had no options other than, figuratively speaking, to throw myself off a cliff with no idea about what might be at the bottom.

I remember the day of the week when I finally broke—it was a Sunday. I was feeling super flat and lost. My emotions felt intense for some reason, and I was not coping with the demons in my mind. These demons made me feel exposed, vulnerable, and worthless. At this stage, I was living with my sister Rachel and her husband, Sam, and I loved both of them. The three of us had a great relationship and I always felt like I could rely on them for anything. Rachel and I had been close most of our lives and, even as adults, we continued having a strong relationship. Sam had been in our lives since I was ten, so needless to say, they were both pretty familiar with and important in my world. Rachel had always been kind, loving, and had acted like my second mum over the years. We had continued to live together once we moved out of our home, and I found comfort in our relationship. She was my best mate, and we had grown up together, going from me being her little shadow and play toy as a child, to not entirely being that close in our teenage years, back to being the best of friends. Up until this point, it seemed crazy that I hadn't found any solace in the idea of telling her my secret. At this stage of her life, she was focused on her relationship with Sam; they had recently been married and were trying for children. I felt like she was always there for me, but maybe she wouldn't understand my dilemma as it was so far removed from her own.

Before this point, both Rachel and Sam had been my rock, and yet in that moment I felt like even my rock might not be stable enough for what was to come. How could I sit in this house and say I was happy when I couldn't even sit within my own self and feel content? I felt like I was in a relationship I couldn't talk about, with a person whose gender I felt I couldn't accept, in a house with people I loved, but a space where I couldn't be myself. Deep down, I knew that my family would be okay, if a little shocked. But my poor mental state kept those rational thoughts away and I was fixated on the potential that I had it all wrong and that they wouldn't accept any of it. I felt like I was a ball of contradictions, lies, and sadness, all ready to explode, and for some reason, Rachel must have been able to see that.

On Sunday nights after the antics of a weekend, we would normally cook a nice roast dinner and have friends or family over to join us. The roast would cook in the late afternoon or early evening while we finished up with weekend chores like washing the car, mowing the lawn, or finishing the laundry. Sundays have always been my favorite day of the week. It feels like a day where both peace and potential exist. You get to switch off, regroup, and prepare for the week ahead. Traditionally, we would cook a roast, have a few laughs around the dinner table, and then all crash onto the couch for some trash TV and banter before bed.

This particular Sunday, after a quiet dinner with just the three of us, I came into the living room from my bedroom in quite a huff. I was feeling flat and agitated with everything. Something was on the TV which wasn't important and my sister and her husband were somewhere between watching whatever was on TV, playing around on their phones and iPads, and chatting away to each other. With no intention of being rude, Rachel made some passing joke at the TV, which happened to have a gay reference. Immediately, it was as if they were having a dig at me. They knew my secret, they were making fun of me, and I could feel myself start to crack.

I knew it. I will be a laughingstock. They think I am a joke now. This is the start of the end. Why did I accept this? Why did I do this? I stormed back into my room. Suddenly aware of my state, Rachel followed behind me.

"What is wrong with you, Luke?" she asked, aware that I wasn't laughing at them like normal.

"Nothing. Get out of my room. I'm fine," I said, a denial as retaliation.

"Nope, I am your sister, and I know when something is wrong. You have been acting strange for a while now, and I can tell you are annoyed at something, but you won't tell me. Just tell me. What is wrong?"

I looked at her, so much emotion inside, dying to just tell her, but I hesitated.

She came and sat next to me on the edge of my bed in the center of the room. The house was a high-set wooden home, traditional to the Queensland region, with wooden floors and wooden walls throughout. My bed was a large brown leather bed that was low to the ground and had a hard leather edge that you could sit on. I would normally have lamps on in my room, as it was nighttime, but for some reason I had the overhead light on. Rachel sat and looked at me. The room felt bright and I felt exposed.

"Nothing," I responded. "How many times do I have to tell you? Why are you on my case all of a sudden? Just leave me alone. I am a big boy; I will be fine."

"Nope, I am not leaving your room until you speak to me. I can stay here all night," she said, with this concerned, but lovingly stubborn smirk on her face.

I looked at her, hesitant to speak as I hadn't even rehearsed this moment. My head started to spin a little, words about to tremble out of my mouth with the power to ruin my life forever. Do I say anything? Do I destroy this amazing relationship by telling her that I am now "one of those gay people"? (Yes, despite having nine months of coming out, my perspective of the gay community was still quite skewed. And yes, we will get to that later in the book!)

"I just… I have to tell you something. But I, I don't know. I just feel stupid." I stumbled over my words.

"Luke, you are not stupid. You know you can always talk to me. Just tell me, what is up?" she pleaded.

"Aghhh… I don't know. I just feel so lost. I need to talk to you about something, but I'm scared. I am scared if I tell you and Mum something—that you will stop loving me!" Tears began to run down my face, and Rachel started to get upset too.

"What? What are you talking about, Luke? I am your sister. I will love you no matter what you tell me," she replied.

There was a pause, only the tears flowing.

"I just… I have been going through a tough time and battling through how I feel about things. And I think, I think I have changed my mind when it comes to who I like? Does that make sense?" I could not even summon the courage to say the words. "I have changed my mind about who I am attracted to… I think I like guys instead. But, I am so scared that you and Mum won't love me if I do!" Tears continue to flow.

Rachel looked at me in shock and grabbed me with both of her hands. "Luke, are you crazy? So what if you are gay? If that is how you feel, then so be it. You are my brother. I love you no matter what. I just *cannot* believe you have been going through this on your own. I am so sorry that you have had to deal with this without me."

Our already heightened emotional state broke and we both began to cry even more. In that moment, a wave of relief rushed over me like nothing I had ever felt before. I had uttered my most significant secret, and the world was still turning. The earth didn't fall off its axis. The moon didn't come crashing out of the sky. And, most importantly, my sister said she still loves me.

We continued to talk for a while. Rachel was asking me how long it has gone on, why I didn't tell her, and if anyone else knew. I was finally able to start speaking honestly about my journey to this point, the darkness that had enveloped me, and my uncertainty about coming out. And as we began to wrap up the conversation, in true sisterly fashion as the tears settled and the energy calmed, right before she got up to leave, she asked, "Sooo… I know it may be a little too soon, but what's your type? Like what men do you like?" We both burst out laughing, and I yelled at her with laughter to get out of the room.

"Too soon, Rachel!" I responded.

The weight of the world lifted from my shoulders. I felt, for the first time, that I could sleep that night with a lighter heart. It was only one person, but it was one of two people who I sincerely cared about for their acceptance. Of course, I care about how all of my family and friends felt, but I knew in my heart that if my sister and my mum didn't accept this, that would have been the hardest reality of all.

The Actual Coming Out

With one of two ladies on board, I had to make some time to speak to my mum. Despite having shared the story with my sister, and feeling some relief, I still had to talk to my mum myself. Knowing the two of them so well, I could only assume that if my sister took it that well, that my mum would be the same. But no matter how many times I told this story, it was always so awkward at the start.

Mum was living in Tasmania at this stage, in the southernmost part of Australia. She had spoken with Rachel, who said I needed some Mum time, and she knew I was in a bad place at the time. She called me and asked if she could fly up for a few days and while she was there, she would do a healing for me. She is qualified in many healing practices, and is the master when it comes to Pellowah healings, a noncontact healing practice that is similar to Reiki, but way more intense.

When she arrived for her stay, I was quieter than normal, but would have been more calm than anything else. I was nervous, but I was trying not to show it. On her first day there, Mum set up her massage table in the spare bedroom and offered me healing. The process only requires you to lie down on your back and close your eyes. It is all energy work that happens around you. I know some people are skeptical of this type of work, but for me it has always seemed to shift or evoke some changes within. I find that Pellowah Healing can cause quite an overwhelming emotional shift during the session. You get crazy images in your mind and feel like the room is so full of energy. Given all that had transpired over the previous nine months, I was in quite a state during the process. In the back of my mind I wondered how I would break the news to Mum.

A day or two had passed since my conversation with Rachel, and I was feeling a little more relaxed about everything, but still wasn't sure what Mum would say about it all.

Once the healing finished, I was in the usual spacey zone that followed and

I sat up on the massage table to debrief the healing with Mum. We were both in a pretty calm place and she looked at me lovingly to see how I was feeling. She pulled up a chair to sit down and chat. In that moment, she gave me this look that said everything was okay; a look that only your mum can offer you.

"Wow, that was intense. You had a lot going on. How was it for you?" Mum asked.

"Yeah, it's been a pretty crazy time of late. I have had a lot going on," I replied.

At the end of every healing, Mum has a word or feeling she offers from the session that she shares with the client to discuss their experience and finish the healing process. For me, she said all she could feel was that her heart was hurting. She felt like my heart was in pain.

"OK. I have to say; I feel like your heart hurts. Your heart is heavy. Has someone hurt you?" Mum asked.

"Yeah, I guess you could say that. No one has hurt me, but I have been in a crazy place in my mind and have lots of thoughts and feelings that have changed over the last year. I need to speak to you about it. You know how I am with all things in my life. Constantly questioning and evaluating what I am doing and where I am going. Well, I have done that with my relationships. And I have realized that maybe I have changed my mind there too," I said, in the most ambiguous manner.

"What do you mean?" Mum asked.

"Like, you know, changed my mind with relationships. [I paused a little longer.] I don't think I like girls anymore," I said.

"Oh, ok. As in, you would rather be with a man instead?" she responded.

As if the words started flooding out of my mouth, I agreed. "Yes… but I have been so scared to tell you and Rachel because I don't want you to stop loving me." Tears welled up in my eyes.

Mum just looked at me and shook her head. "Luke, you have made me, and continue to make me, more proud than you will ever understand. Nothing you do would ever stop me from loving you. And if you have decided that you like blokes instead, then so be it. It doesn't mean my love for you will be any less."

We both cried and hugged one another. We chatted for a bit and then Mum had one more piece of advice for me.

"All I can ask of this world for you Luke is that you are happy," she said. "But if there was one thing I don't want you to forget, it is that your sexuality, while it may feel overwhelming now, is not only who you are. You are still the same person as you were before— this is just a part of you. Who you decide to sleep with behind closed doors is your prerogative, but it does not define you. Please do not forget that."

I sat there for a minute processing what she said. What I took from those words my mum said to me that day was nothing other than profoundness. And those words have stuck with me over the years, and continue to hold with me now. In fact, they are part of the baseline for this book: Your sexuality is absolutely part of you, but it does not define you. Stay truthful to the values that you hold, and remember that you are so much more than who you decide to sleep with, and who you choose to love.

When I was reflecting on this moment in my life, I spoke with Mum and asked how she felt about the situation. Many of her own thoughts reflect our shared experience, but she did say that it was a good shake-up for her own values and ideals;

"This experience, while I met it with love, of course, came with a good shake-up for me. I found myself, as his mother, still wondering the same things—what about children? Marriage? White picket fence? How would I overcome this? Well, I was the one who had to change my thoughts on what his life should be. It is his life after all, and it is his story to make. What I have learned out of all of this is that those same dreams are possible, regardless of sexuality. It is just a matter of perspective.

In the following months of learning this new information, I decided the only way to resolve this was to shift my thoughts and belief to create a new version for myself. This old belief system I had required an upgrade, and what better time to do it than now? And at the end of the day, all I wanted was for him to be a happy and healthy man who did whatever his heart desired. I told him this from a young age, and it wasn't going to change now. My love for him has never wavered, it has only become more full."

The relief I had felt once my Mum and sister were on board was unbelievable. I knew I cared for them and how they felt about me, but I never imagined how much of an impact that acceptance was going to have on this journey. It was almost as if once I had their blessing, I felt like I was unstoppable. OK—maybe more so with hindsight, but at the time it was unquestionably energizing. Now that I was comfortable with actually beginning this new journey, I knew I had to let other people know too.

It is such a funny thing, "coming out." This need to walk around and do what no other heterosexual person has had to do: exclaim to the world who I have decided to sleep with and who I have decided to love. I mean, this may be the society we live in, but what business is it to anyone else? To me, I was breaking the social norm and almost having to put myself out to ask that people will still love the same guy they did before, knowing that he is now choosing to love a man and not a woman. It was like I was a defective toy that was just asking not to be thrown out.

I decided that, like all things in life, I was just going to own it. As long as the two most important people in my world still love me, then if I lose some people, or get some "battle wounds" along the way, I don't care. I was in the darkest place of my life up until this point, and now I was so desperate to get on with it and just be happy.

Game Plan
Now I was comfortable with my decision; I decided that I would hit up this next step in the process with a bit of a game plan—a strategy, if you will. I went through my life and, in my head, created a circle of my immediate friends; those who matter to me and whom I have so much love and respect for. I needed to approach the situation with the same love and respect in return. Over a two-week period, as it happened, I decided that I would find some time to either catch up in person or call (if they didn't live in the same city), and let them know that a few things had changed for me. I wanted to tell them myself that the old Luke, while he may have changed in the process, was now back from this nine months of labor. For many of my friends, I felt I had become distant as I was pulling away from so many people. How could I be a good friend when I couldn't be open and honest like I had always been?

This game plan worked. I set up dinners with some of my best mates in the first week, one-on-one, to catch up and let them in on what has been happening. I began with one of my closest friends, Beth. As I mentioned, we had been friends since I was in Grade 11 and we had lived in London and traveled through Europe together. Since coming back to Australia, Beth had gone on her own journey and our friendship had changed slightly. Mostly this was as a result of the changes I had undergone over the past nine months, but during that time Beth also met the man whom she would eventually marry. As she and I were quite close, I imagined she would be a supporter of this new information, as many members of her family always thought she and I would end up together.

I recall meeting Beth for dinner, not long after I had spoken to Rachel and Mum. We went to the local Nepalese restaurant in Red Hill that I used to frequent when I was craving delicious Nepalese cuisine. The restaurant was in an old "Queenslander," which is the style of house we lived in, but it was bigger than our house. When we arrived, we were taken to our usual table which included floor seating (a very authentic and novel experience, until halfway through the dinner when your legs go to sleep and you have to keep moving every five minutes to wake them up). We sat down, ordered our momos (dumplings) and Dal Bhat (the staple meal throughout Nepal, eaten twice daily), and began our usual chitchat. Beth knew something was up, and she said I was far quieter than normal. I wasn't quite sure how to approach the subject. While I knew she would be supportive and that she was in a new relationship, I couldn't ignore the fact that we had our own history. Even as best mates, we had shared some really intimate and personal experiences over the years. To sit down and come out with something that was so big at the time was a huge deal for me. I had always prided myself on my communication skills, and I didn't see why this had to be any different.

As I began to speak, Beth told me to get straight to the point. She could see that I was tiptoeing around a subject and started to prod me a bit. She said she could tell that something had been up, especially in the last few weeks, and she was concerned for me. This was as good an opportunity as any. I started to explain to Beth about how things had changed and that I had been on my own journey when the tears began to flow. I couldn't seem to hold it in. I told her that I was gay and that I had been in a really dark place for the last few months. She, too, began to get upset. I remember her watching me speak so intently, so as not to miss a single word.

When Beth talks about this conversation now, she recalls initially being worried that she had done something wrong and I was about to tell her what it was. Once she realized that wasn't the case, she said she intuitively felt that I was about to come out to her, but that she didn't want it to be true because personally, and selfishly (as she admits), she doesn't like dealing with change. But when I finally told her, she said she felt a feeling of warmth come over her. She felt content to see that a weight had been lifted from my shoulders and suddenly everything began to make sense; my poor record of holding down relationships with girls, my lack of commitment, and the fact that she and I had such a close relationship. To her, these things didn't make sense and the reality allowed them to settle in her mind.

We sat and spoke for a couple of hours. Funnily enough, we hadn't done that for a long time, just sat and spent time together. It was so nice. I remember we kept crying randomly throughout the evening, which made for a few awkward yet hilarious moments with the Nepalese servers, but it actually brought us even closer together. I was allowed to be myself with another soul who loved me, just for being me. I hadn't experienced this type of calm before. It wasn't just calm in my mind, but deep in my soul. One thing I will always remember is that Beth said the one thing she appreciated was that I took the time and care with all my words to ensure that I was loving and compassionate when sharing this information with her. She knew I had been in a bad place, but I'd had nine months of dealing with this. By taking the time to sit, explain, and allow the space to talk, it allowed for her to completely take in my story and be there for me in any way she could. This, above all else, mattered the most to me.

As we left, I gave her a massive hug and thanked her for being such a great friend. Beth recalls leaving the venue and suddenly being hit with a new wave of emotions—realization of change that was taking place, potential for change in our relationship, within me, and within the perceptions of her family. Without knowing it, she began on her own journey of accepting this new information. This wasn't a bad thing, but it wasn't expected, and it just goes to show how important it was that I allowed for this time to sit with her and reconnect.

For the rest of my close friends who I had quite a history with, my story received the same response as it did from my mum and sister. Tears of sadness from the fact that I had battled alone, followed by kind words of acceptance and love. I know for them, they each reacted in the way that respected me, but they also had to find space to reflect on it themselves. As for them, while it wasn't going to impact their worlds, they, too, had their dreams and ideas for me. Whether we like it or not, we all think we know someone, and as such, we create these expectations in our mind of where they will end up and with whom they will end up. And this happens so naturally for all of us, that with this type of news it almost forces us back to have to rethink this identity we have built for them and for ourselves.

With each conversation I had, I would become a little more comfortable. I was able to choose different words to describe my recent change in life and slowly got closer to saying those, at that time, three dreaded words—"I am gay." For those who don't have to do this, it is really hard to say the words if you are coming from a place, where for so long, you denied it even to yourself. The nice part for my ego was that I had only one friend who did drop the line, "Yeah, I thought this might be the case." The last thing you want to hear is "I knew it" or "I told you so." Especially when you are coming to terms with your sexuality, and you genuinely believe that you did not know this was going to happen. If you are friends with someone coming out, and maybe you did know it, trust me, now is not the time to share your amazing insights. Just be kind and allow them to share their story.

After two weeks of catching up with friends and filling them in on the story of my authentic self, I was feeling pretty good about life. I felt like I was finding my feet, understanding my new identity, and, for the first time in a year, had hope again. It is incredible just how dark that space becomes when you are so alone. My family was all coming to terms with it, not in a terrible way, just in a funny way. My mum would say things like, "Oh, is this umm, your new mate?" if we were talking about a guy I met or was dating. I would respond with, "Mum, you can say "boyfriend"… and no, he is not." She would get so flustered, bless her, and would say she just didn't know what to call it as she wasn't sure how I felt. That type of kindness added some humor to the process and did make me ease into the new dialogue.

Once I had come out to everyone else, I felt like I was OK and could just update people as we go. It wasn't long before Christmas when this all happened, and we were off on a family Christmas trip to New York that year. My brother, Lee, and I were traveling together and would meet my sister and brother-in-law in NYC. Lee—who was living in Adelaide at the time, clear across the country from me—and I decided we would go to LA first, and then Vegas, before heading over and joining them. It was going to be an epic trip. However, there was one small issue: I had yet to tell him I was gay. I knew it wouldn't be an issue or change anything, but for me, it was the big old elephant just banging around in the room the whole time, until I found the right moment to let him know. Now, most of you probably think I chose to do it before we left. Or even on the aircraft. Or, maybe at dinner one night. Nope, I decided during a deep and meaningful conversation while driving on a seven-lane freeway in LA that right *then* would be a good time to have the discussion. It was so funny; he had no idea what I was trying to say until I said it. Then his reaction was priceless. "Oh, you like blokes. OK… (pause). I was not expecting that… (pause). Honestly, I would have expected Jay (our other brother) before you."

We both started laughing. Sorry, Jay. (He has heard this story plenty of times.) It took him a few days to get his head around it and stop trying to get me to pick up girls when we were out, but it didn't stop us from having an awesome time together.

The one person I didn't tell myself, but still had a conversation with after, was my dad. After everything that had gone on in life, I never felt super close to him. He's my dad, I love him, and I have learned a lot from him, but it wasn't going to make or break me whether he accepted or not. As terrible as that may sound, I believe, irrelevant of whether you are family or not, my respect has to be earned as much as I expect others' respect to be gained by me. And if I lacked in that department, my desire to tell you was probably not there. Mum decided to take it upon herself and tell him. He called me afterward, without knowing that he was aware, and said to me, "Mate, your mother told me about everything. I just want you to know that you are my son and I love you no matter what." That statement, offered with as much love and kindness as he knew how to, meant the world to me, even if I thought I didn't need it in the first place.

The Coming-out Relationship Continued

After going through this tremendous personal change, I felt a renewed sense of power and hope. I felt like I had been hiding the best version of myself for so long, and it was time to dust him off and bring him back out even more fabulous than before. Over the time of coming out to family and friends, I was still seeing the same guy. He was a great sounding board to speak to and share my stories with as I unveiled my authentic self. The relationship, however, began to strain. It wasn't that anything had changed from his side, it was that my whole world was changing. I no longer had to hide the fact that I was seeing this guy. I no longer had to sneak off to his house and spend time without people knowing. I could finally start creating the type of relationship I wanted—one that was open and loving and built on growth and authenticity. But it seemed that wouldn't work. The relationship began to break down as the old Luke no longer accepted things that he had never seen before. I stopped accepting weird mood swings, jealous outbursts, and distrustful behavior, not to mention the belief that we had to hide our relationship from some people. There were fractures in the foundation of what we had created and with good reason. It was a relationship built at a time when I was not authentically myself, and as such accepted things that did not necessarily align with what my ideal expectations of a relationship would. Now that isn't to say that he was doing anything wrong, it was that I was accepting everything in the wrong way. The relationship no longer fit the person I felt I was and the person I looked to become, and as such, we had to bring it to an end.

What I learned from this relationship and experience was the importance of authenticity. Accepting something as personal as a relationship with another person when you are not authentically yourself is detrimental to your own self-worth. When it comes to love, irrelevant of sexuality, many of us do this. We don't believe that we are worthy of the true love we so deeply deserve.

In my situation, this is no one's fault but my own. For many people, their own relationship with their authentic selves, irrelevant of sexuality, creates this same situation when it comes to love. They simply don't believe that they are worthy of anything greater than what other people say they are worthy of. And so, they accept what is offered. And we all do it. We fear that the love we need is not going to come our way, and so we accept whatever the next person can give, without thinking whether it truly meets our needs. Knowing I had done this myself, I stepped away from this relationship and into a new world.

THE COMING-OUT LESSONS

Given how important and pivotal this particular period of my life was, I couldn't have offered just one or two simple lessons. I know that for many people, this period can be daunting, destructive, and quite a dark time. But it doesn't have to be. Whether I am being an idealist or a thought leader, it is up to the individual, but I thought I would offer six of the most important lessons I took away from this significant time in my life:

1. The timing will never be perfect.

This seems to be one thing that I hear from many people who I meet that have either not come out yet or are in the process of it. When you speak to them and ask why they haven't done it yet, the response is usually that the timing hasn't been right. I can tell you now; it won't ever be the "right" time for you to have to come to terms with the actual feelings of your sexuality, and feel that you have to explain yourself to your friends or family. But, that doesn't mean you put it off. The only thing that isn't right is your fear of what will come. I appreciate that for some people, this can still be a highly dramatic time with the consequences unknown, but if you were to die tomorrow, and by accepting yourself in full meant you were able to lead an even more significant and more authentic life, why would you ever procrastinate on that? The timing will never work for everyone, but figure out when it works for you, and the universe will have your back for the rest.

2. Everyone's reaction is different, and it is usually more about them than it is about you.

This applies to most things in life, but the responses of those around you are merely that of their values and perspective. Some people couldn't care less about the whole situation, while others will force their opinion on you, or dismiss you, as you no longer fit in the box they have imagined for you. The main reminder throughout this process is to know that their reaction is more about them than it is about you. Stay focused on finding your authentic self—and if that means losing some people along the way, then so be it. It will be their loss should they not find the courage to love you as you are and as you have always been.

3. Experience is everything, but know your limitations.

I speak quite candidly about the many different experiences that I had during my time of coming out. I do this because I want to openly describe the reality for many when it comes to this exploration of sexuality. For me, I was learning that I had the makings of a highly sexual person who had apparently not been looking in the right places. Before this I thought something was wrong with me, as that part of my being was never truly ignited. So it's no wonder at first, I was a little obsessive about getting my fix. This doesn't mean that going out and sleeping with lots of people is the answer, though! It was just the journey that was written for me. For many other people, you may only have a few sexual partners in your life, and that is okay, too, as your journey may be about uncovering other aspects of yourself. What I did learn is that the experience of so many partners was part of my journey to understand my own internal emotions and desires. I had particular urges and feelings that I could only learn by experiencing them. And had I been close to those who had encountered it themselves and could have explained it to me from their own experience, I may have skipped the silly behavior and got on with other things. So, I say, experience what you need to and know your limitations. I may have tried something that I thought worked for me, but that doesn't mean every person should try it.

4.   Offer those closest to you the respect and time they need to hear it.
Looking back on my experience of coming out, this is one area where I feel quite proud of my response. One of my most significant concerns was that those who were nearest and dearest to me would reject my newfound sense of self. I was worried, despite having known these people—friend and family—for many years, that they would push me away or choose not to be the friend I thought they were. Even after saying that I learned that you might lose some people, I wanted to know that I did all I could first to ensure that they could hear my story and understand what I have been through, rather than learn from social hearsay. To do this, I chose to create a space for us to share and for me to explain to them in person. This wasn't some plea for them to love me, this was a sign of respect for our friendship. If I could offer any advice to others in this same place, it would be to sit with those who matter most to you and offer them the respect they deserve to hear your story. It may have been a traumatic and challenging time for you, but you have been through the journey already; they haven't. Give those who matter to you a space to sit and hear your story, offer their own words of love and support in return, and find their peace in this new situation. And should anything change as a result of this, you know that you did all you could.

5.   You are not alone.
This is the most critical point I want to make: No matter how dark that mind gets, no matter how hard it feels, no matter how much you feel like you are a failure or that you are doing something "wrong" in the eyes of others, know that you are NOT ALONE. For centuries, men and women have battled the same reality. A reality set by an outdated perspective that we believe "society" holds and one that is changing every day. A reality that makes us believe that we are so different or that we are not enough. But we are not different, and we are more than enough. We are honoring our authentic selves, we are

choosing to accept who we are and who we cannot change, and we own our place in the world for us to love and to be loved in return. My story is an opportunity to remind you that you are not alone; a chance to show others the difficulty people face coming to terms with their sexuality every day; and an opportunity for us all to know that this is normal. It is not some abnormality amongst a small group of people. It is part of our human makeup, to which we are all the same. As the queen herself, Lady Gaga, says, "Baby, you were born this way."

6. **<u>Know that the authentic you is more powerful than you can imagine.</u>**

Not only are you not alone, you are also in a time of incredible transformation. You can't see it now, but like a butterfly in a cocoon, you are changing shape and features to turn into the most beautiful, authentic version of yourself. The difficulty we experience in such a turbulent time of our lives is being able to see our future selves for what we will become. We are battling daily with accepting who we are and allowing ourselves to transform into the life we want to lead. But if we could just sit back, away from fear, and imagine the self that we will become, I promise it would take you from fear to ecstasy. Once you finally go through your process, in whatever time and capacity it takes, I promise you that you will be a fuller and more fulfilled person. The power that comes with authenticity is beyond what any of us can imagine. And for many people who have been in a world of uncertainty for so long, coming out into your skin is a liberation that only you will understand once you have been through it.

I knew deep down that this would be an arduous journey. Some of the experiences I had not prepared myself for, but what can we plan for in life? It is all about the magic of the experience. What I do know for sure is that by the end of this transformation, I found out who I was, I found out who my friends and family were, and I found out that living a limited life will always cause you to feel unsettled and lost. It is our duty in this human existence not only to find what relationship we have with God or our community, but first and foremost to find what relationship we have with ourselves. For we are the beginning of all of our experiences, and it is our responsibility to be as authentic to ourselves as possible—free from conditions and expectations, and open to love and be loved in whatever capacity we see fit. For when we die, our spirit will not take the social conditions and expectations with it, rather our soul will hold on and treasure the experience and love we have managed to find and create in our life.

THE ALL-CONSUMING LOVE

Once you align with your authentic self, you find that you start to see not only hope in your world, but a more explicit vision of your future self. It is as if once you are back in the light, you can see, subconsciously, who you are truly capable of being. It takes a while to be able to understand this, and to find a way to manage that picture so that it is not distorted—but your emotional reactions, your desires, and your expectations are all set to this new life path.

Stepping out from the darkness of my "coming out," I not only had new desires and expectations when it came to love, but I had a zest for life when it came to meeting people. I was hungry to make up for what time I felt I had lost. As all things go, after ending my "coming-out relationship," the universe gave me someone very quickly, who represented so much more than my first intense love. It gave me someone, who, with the incredible ability of hindsight, was a reflection of all the things I desired, and a vision of how my future love would look. This realization is not to say that I didn't feel these things for him, without a doubt I did—but looking back he quite literally reminds me of the man I am with now!

This story is about the all-consuming love. The love that we seem to find, in a time when we least expect it. The one that may be short or long, but holds more lessons than you could imagine.

For the sake of this story and not calling people by name, I am going to tell you about a guy whose name is, let's say, Jake. Jake was living in Australia on a working holiday, but not originally from here. He came into my life via my favorite people resource at the time, Grindr. I had arrived back into Sydney early from the US, as I was run-down and tired from a massive Christmas trip. During my quick stopover in Sydney, I must have gone online, or the app was on in the background, and as it is location-based, picked up his profile on my way through. I got back to Brisbane, and that evening, went online to chat with people before bed. Jake popped up saying hi, and I was immediately interested. He was handsome, had a great body, and good chat. I was like, "Hello, my little welcome back treat." As soon as we were chatting, I was hoping that I would be able to sneak out and maybe see him in person. As it turns out, that wasn't going to happen, as he was in Sydney. Ugh, always the way!

We started chatting and ended up getting along really well. One thing led to another, and we swapped numbers, rather than keep speaking via the app. We started with texting, and quite quickly moved to calling each other. I remember hearing his voice for the first time. It was this super cute Canadian accent that I used to laugh at and say that he sounded a bit like Yogi Bear. He didn't, but it was fun to say while flirting. Before I knew it, we were into deep conversations about life and love, and everything in between. For the first time, I had met someone who had so much depth of character. And I was not only attracted to a guy for his looks, but I was so deeply attracted to the type of conversation and connection we had. He couldn't be real! I was immediately captivated. But, I remember thinking how stupid I must be. How could I be so interested in this guy that I have never met?

The "itch" to meet was intense. We needed to see each other. Immediately we started planning a trip for him to Brisbane. I decided I could fly him up on my staff travel benefits (perks of working for an airline), we could book somewhere for the weekend and hang out. One thing led to another, and before we knew it, he was coming up to Brisbane. Except, after all that scheming I decided just to ask him to stay at my house. To this day, I have no idea what story I had told my sister and her husband, who I lived with, as to how I knew this guy. But I had this gut feeling that I couldn't shake, that it will all be ok. At the time, I assumed it was just sexual, but once I met him, I found out it wasn't. We set a date, and he was on his way.

When he arrived at my house in the inner-city suburbs of Brisbane, I was nervous to meet him. I mean, we had been chatting this whole time, but without my family knowing, I hadn't met him in person before. But for some reason, I was okay with this arrangement up until now. But then here he was, arriving at my place. As his car pulled up, I walked out the front door along the path to the street that ran along the front side of the house to meet him. I recall seeing him and thinking that he looked exactly as I imagined, although he was a little shorter than I expected, but still just as handsome. He was from a mixed cultural background; he had Caribbean features, olive skin, short shaved hair, a fit body, and lovely eyes. His kind voice emanated the warmth of his energy. He felt as nice as he looked. And it was as if we had been old friends who were reunited for the first time in a long time. We exchanged hugs, and I invited him in. He immediately got along with my family and brought an energy into the house that was completely trustworthy. Well, I hoped he was as I was about to share my bed with this complete stranger for a few days. The first night we went to bed I remember rolling over and saying to him, "I feel like I know you already. I feel like we have been apart for a long time and finally, we get to come back together." The feeling was mutual and undeniable, and it set the tone for his stay with us for the next few days. To say they were an intense few days would be an understatement.

Jake had been in Australia for the past year as he had come on a working holiday visa. He was obsessed with visiting "down under" and finally had the opportunity to make it happen. During his stay, he said he met some amazing people and spent a large portion of his time in Sydney. He also went down to Melbourne, where he did a ten-day silent meditation retreat. This type of spontaneous and free-spirited attitude, mixed with his interest in finding himself spiritually, resonated with me and my own experiences. I gravitated toward him and we connected. Yet in all of this, there was one "catch." He told me he was already in a relationship back home, albeit they weren't in a great place when he left, and that he wanted to come and hang out, but only as friends for now. I felt so strongly toward him that I accepted that and still said he should come visit. Maybe I considered it more of a challenge, given my lack of interest in relationships and the somewhat selfish headspace I was in, but I did agree for him to come, nonetheless. Over his stay, we had a few up-and-down moments. For me, there were these uncomplicated moments of bliss. We would lie on my bed during the day when it was pouring down with rain, and we would laugh and talk about every part of life, and maybe share the occasional kiss. He was a deep thinker, and at the time, I was missing this type of dialogue in my world. We would sit at the end of my bed and talk about life, love, authenticity, the value of family, finding your purpose—the list went on. At times I recall him looking at me, getting a little emotional, and saying something like, "Hey, when did you learn how to chat like this?"

There were two moments I recall that I felt my heart soar beyond any expectation I ever had in my love life.

The first was when we were in our living room on our couch, which was this round love seat, with my sister and brother-in-law. He and I were sitting together on this loveseat, watching TV and chatting with the others. Everyone just seemed to be so comfortable. And for the first time, I was too. I looked at this man, who appeared out of nowhere, and saw exactly the type of person that I had only ever dreamt about sitting right in front of me. Without knowing it, I had these ideas already in my mind about how my ideal partner would look; the shape of his face, his eyes, his beard, his body type, even his cultural background. These were all attributes I imagined for my partner. I never imagined anyone who looked like me, but rather someone from a completely different background. But were these traits that made up my partner who I "thought" I wanted to be with? Or was it a really close image of what my future partner would look like? Depends on your perspective, I guess.

The second moment was toward the end of the trip when I took him to our usual beach spot in Coolum, a beach town north of Brisbane. As he visited during the summer, the weather was perfect and this particular day was ideal for the beach. So, I packed up the car, put the dogs in the back, and headed north to the beach, just he and I. As we arrived, the spot was pretty quiet as it is normally frequented more by locals than day-trippers. We parked the car on the residential street, grabbed the dogs and our towels, and made our way along the sand path that runs between the bushland that lay before the beach. As we got closer to the beachfront, the ocean surge got louder and as we followed the path, we were led to the top of some steps that took us down to the beach. Standing at the top of the stairs, we had a view over the whole section of the beach. The waves were alive and met our gaze; the turquoise and aqua colors mixed together in the different depths of the water and the white foamy sea spray provided a border as it crashed down onto the ocean. The sun was hot and bright above us, but the breeze was somehow still a little cool. As we reached the beach, to the left of the stairs was a massive pandanus tree, which is native to that part of the coast. This particular tree sat right on the beach and provided the perfect spot for shade during a hot summer day. My friends and family always sit by this tree when they are at this beach, so it felt even more special to set up here with him.

Once we were settled, the dogs went ballistic and started running like crazy on the beach. We headed down to the water and dove in. The water was the perfect temperature—enough to cool you down from the darker waters below while still being a little warm from the summer sun. As we were in the water, he swam over to me and we got a little closer while we took in the perfect day. It was as if I could see his guard starting to come down and the connection we had was growing. I know for me this experience was only making it harder to not want to be with this guy. I had been living in emotional darkness for the last nine months and all of a sudden, the realization that I could be so comfortably me and share it with this incredible man who felt like a manifestation of my dreams, was surreal. It sounds crazy now, but the reality of experiencing something I didn't think would be possible was overwhelming. At one stage, whether it was the heat from the sun, or a mutual desire, we locked bodies in the water and kissed. And in that moment, in that sweet moment of connection and intimacy, I felt more alive than I had in a very long time.

As the day went on, we moved between lying on the beach, swimming in the ocean, and sitting in the branches of the pandanus tree and laughing. It was pure bliss.

This time with him was not only being spent with someone, that in my mind, was an image of who I felt I would "end up with," but was also the first time when I felt so genuinely free in love. I was finally with a gorgeous man, who I didn't have to lie about, at my favorite beach that my family and I go to, just being ourselves and having fun. And most of all, I felt like I was in love. I felt like this is what the storybooks were telling us. A time when your expectations and reality are so aligned, it is almost an out-of-body experience. You don't know what to do with it.

Outside of those two memorable moments, the rest of our time was spent hanging out, going to the movies, exploring Brisbane, and getting to know one another. It was a bittersweet visit which he extended by a few days. I would find myself getting caught up in the moment and then remembering that he was not from here, he was due to head back home soon, and most importantly, he was already committed to someone else. These realizations hurt more as the week went on, and I found myself demanding his time more and more, just to see if he would give it to me, which was unhealthy. As I was looking to move out of Sam and Rach's house, he came along to look at a few places with me. This was the ultimate test, as I found myself asking him to stay on longer and stay with me in my new place.

He was so kind about it all. He completely recognized that we had a connection and loved his time with me and my family, but he struggled when I asked him to stay longer or change his own circumstances to see what we might have together. It was unfair of me to have done that, but I was so overwhelmed with my own emotions that I could barely consider why he wouldn't feel the same way. Equally, I could see that he was torn and felt like maybe he would see it in the same way as I did.

The Luke of that time would love to say that we lived happily ever after, much as I had dreamed of doing with my high school sweetheart. But that wasn't how the story would go. In fact, it went from a joyful bliss to a reality of heartache. This heartache was partially self-inflicted and partially not. Despite all the warning signs and knowing he had a boyfriend back home, a deluded part of me felt that I could change that. How could this love that we were feeling and this connection we shared, not get us through this, and we stay together? He was all the things I felt like I wanted in a partner. How could we not continue on this fairy tale? As much as I kept ignoring it, and although he did extend his stay, I knew he had to leave in the end. And the day he did, my heart broke. Not for the first time, but for a love I hadn't felt before. Although, it goes without saying that my hope didn't fade immediately. I felt like this was not going to be the last time we saw each other and that our story was only beginning. This relationship though, was one I kept throwing myself into, only to find it led down a path of heartache. I would see myself pleading on the phone for him to come back so we could find a way to be together. He didn't help things by continuing these conversations, but it was my persistence that created most of my pain.

After he left, I had worked myself up to such a point that I created another of the most vulnerable moments I recall in love. I was so heartbroken and missed him so much that I decided I would go and see him. If he couldn't afford to come to me, I would go to him. I called him one day, and we had an intense conversation. I decided to tell him that I want him to know how much I want this, that I will get on a flight in a week's time to come to the USA, and he could do the same, and we can meet up and talk about this in person. I said I didn't need to know anything more than an OK for me to come. Even if it meant leaving without any plans to be together, I just needed to see him again. To wear my heart on my sleeve would have been a more protected stance for me to take than what I was attempting at that moment. Despite the universe pushing back at me, I was not only simply putting myself out there for the chance to win this relationship—I was putting myself into the ultimate space of vulnerability with maybe a bit of sheer stupidity sprinkled on top.

He paused. He was panicked. He followed the silence up with a "no." He said he couldn't do it, and that he couldn't have me fly over to him, in the midst of him feeling so lost with everything. He asked for more time and for me not to go anywhere, but ultimately he couldn't give me what I wanted.

I was heartbroken.

Quite literally, broken.

I remember finishing the conversation abruptly. Throwing my mobile phone across the lounge room and falling to the ground in a fetal position bawling my eyes out. Why did this hurt so much? Why did I see such hope, only for him to not be part of this? Why am I such an idiot? Why did I put myself out there like this just to be rejected so bluntly? Why didn't he love me the way I wanted him too? *I hate him*, I thought. But I didn't, and that is what hurt the most. I promised not to speak to him again. That, too, didn't happen. Our contact continued for a period, even into my next relationship. I couldn't quite let him go. I knew it wouldn't go anywhere, but I just couldn't drop my contact with him. Maybe my pride was hurt too much, that the idea of cutting him off completely would have exacerbated it further. Or perhaps I just knew we were unfinished. Either way, our connection and the merry-go-round between us continued. Not with anywhere near as much energy, but still ticking over, like an app in the background of your smartphone.

Over time, I began to understand the relationship in more depth. It took a while to get there, but like all things, sometimes you just need time. With time came the understanding that these types of relationships happen to so many of us. It was the all-consuming love that I had to experience after coming into my own skin for the first time. The turbulent emotions were just the effects of this new chemical explosion in my body. For others who experience the same thing, this might be your first love, or it may be the first love that has met the fairy tale that you have created in your mind. Either way, it is consuming and takes your head into this space where you think that life could not offer you anything better than what you have found, even if it is not reciprocated. And sadly, in order to keep it, you find yourself compromising many of your core values. Allowing someone who is with another person to come and stay with you, quite intimately, and be part of your world, all while they lie on your bed and message their current partner, is not okay. Not because we are questioning others' views of an open relationship, but because it is not representative of the value of your own self-worth in that moment. Why was I sitting there and allowing myself to be the "other" person? Why was I allowing myself to fall for a man who was already taken? Why was I trying to convince someone to love me? Was it his fault? Of course not. I am in control of my own actions and reactions. Therefore, if I allowed this to happen, that speaks volumes about how I perceive myself. And understandably so, given the recent changes that had taken place in my life.

Despite these feelings and realizations, I look back on this relationship with such gratitude. It was tough at the time, and it took a long time to get here, but the love I felt with this man, the connection, the image of my future self—it was all for a far more significant reason. It was for me to understand that the "ideal" I had in my mind, in this new skin I had found, does exist. This may not be the reality for me, which is hard to understand in the moment, but if I could experience this with this man, then who says that out of the eight billion other people on the planet, I wasn't going to find one who held all of these attributes? And seeing that I am now in a healthy relationship with a man who has exceeded even my current-day expectations and created a life with me that is beyond my own wildest dreams, I know this to be true. However, even before I met my current champion (more about him later), I knew that the spiritual contract I had with Jake was complete and the lesson had been learned. If it hadn't been, I would never had been in a space to meet this new man. Learning and accepting the lessons were two different things.

This love showed me how important it is **not to compromise** on your core values when it comes to finding the right partner. I look back, and I see the information provided to me and the actions that took place, and I can see that I was not only forcing a love to take place in the language that only I understood, but I was willing to compromise on my values to have it. Compromising on things like being the "other" person, accepting only what I could get from this guy, and not being in a position of believing that I deserved all he could offer, diminished my self-worth. Looking back, I am so glad this didn't go anywhere. I was not ready for the love it could have been, nor did I understand the love that I was capable of offering. I was seeking a profound love from a man who was already in a relationship, and yet I didn't truly know what this profound love looked like from my side. I had not yet learned how to love myself properly, let alone another person in the way my fairy-tale mind was hoping.

When I reminisce about this relationship, the challenges I faced, and my own struggle with accepting it for what it was, I believe I was most fearful of not finding love like this again. This wouldn't be the last time I felt this way. We all do it! We fear we are not worthy; we buy into scarcity, and we accept our limitations are real. It is a shame, but it's a common reality in love. Every one of us has had a relationship like this; we may even be in a relationship like this where we just can't seem to let go, even if the universe is telling us otherwise. But what I have learned is that if the winds of life are battling against you, shift your mast. The universe is telling you to keep moving. You will find love. You are worthy of something far greater than what you perceive. And your value is not determined by that situation. The real problem is that you are just looking in the wrong place.

As for Jake, he knows who he is. And he knows that the love we shared was real. I am genuinely grateful for this, and will always remember our all-consuming love story that shaped me into the person I am today.

CREATING LOVE IN A NEW WORLD

After my last intense love story, I was battered and confused, not quite sure where to look or how to feel. I didn't know if I wanted to hide away from love or keep searching for it. As it was so early on in my new world of love, my desires for more kept me moving forward, despite having a broken heart. To not lose sight of the road ahead, my next incredible connection was placed in front of me very quickly. A man whom I had a sincere desire to understand and to learn about, from the moment we connected. My newest "itch" in life.

At the time I was working for Virgin Australia. I had managed to get myself there through a background in the travel industry and as a result of knowing the manager of the team from my previous job. I sent her a Facebook message one night, asking if she had any jobs available. I don't know what made me do it, I guess it was another "itch," but she happened to have vacancies at the time. She invited me for an interview, and within a few weeks I started my new job. The role was in the "staff & duty travel" team, which managed the benefits and corporate travel for the airline. I started as a coordinator, and was promoted to team leader within six months.

It was around February, and I was still getting over my heartbreak. Time frames between the two were short, but as I said, I was determined to just get on with things rather than wallow in self-pity. I was at work one day and sitting at the desk of a good friend of mine, Lorraine (we call her Loz)—the same friend who inadvertently introduced me to Grindr a year or so before. We were roaring with laughter, as we did most days, which helped us to get through the monotony of the corporate world. In between topics, she asked if I had met the new guy, let's call him "Dan," who was in Product.

"No… should I?" I responded.

She told me to keep an eye out for him, and he was wearing a pink shirt. We continued our antics before I went back to my desk. As I got back to my office, I looked outside to see a guy walk past in a pink shirt. *Could that be him?* I thought. I picked up my work phone and called Loz.

"I think I saw him. Yes, he's lovely. Please bring him to my desk immediately," I said, hanging up the phone in a flurry of excitement. Fifteen minutes later, he was standing next to my desk with Lorraine.

For those that don't know, when it comes to the airline world, you want to know the staff-travel team, as we were the immediate go-to for everyone's flight or hotel issues. We're like the in-house corporate travel agents, if you will. Loz told him that he has to know me, as he will travel a lot, and so she brought him down for a meet and greet. I acted super professional, albeit a little stuck for words; I was more than a little distracted by his brown puffy chest showing itself out of his fitted work shirt. After our meeting, he sent an email, and I responded. A little flirting pursued and before you know it, we were on. "Shall we do a little dinner next week when I am in town?" he asked. I loved how confident he seemed and was on board. Dinner went well and ended with a kiss. The following trip after he got back, he invited me over to his apartment for some late-night wine and cheese, as we had both been busy. As the evening continued, our chatting led to kissing again. And that led to me leaving first thing the next morning. He was super nervous to do anything, as he had been through his own recent journey of change and was hesitant to get mixed up with anyone. He had his own personal challenges and was quite vulnerable. I think, despite loving the confidence he had up front, this vulnerability was even more attractive to me. The puffy chest and good looks were one thing, but knowing that he had this kind heart beneath was a win for me. The evening connected us and we continued to spend time together each week when he came to Brisbane for work. Before you know it, we started dating. I wasn't quite sure what I was doing, as, well, it was my first real "gay" relationship. He was from Sydney and lived in Darlinghurst, the absolute epicenter of the Australian gay community. Darlinghurst is located in the heart of Sydney, just outside the main CBD and Oxford Street; a main thoroughfare that runs from the CBD out to Bondi (the coast in Sydney) runs right through it. Oxford Street is known for its nightclubs and nightlife and has a reputation for being the "gay district" in Sydney. Oxford Street is where the annual Gay and Lesbian Mardi Gras is held, which is one of the biggest in the world. Needless to say, given its reputation, and location, it is home to a large population of the gay community, which is refreshing. I, on the other hand, lived a polar opposite life in suburban Brisbane, surrounded by families and young couples looking to buy their first home. And at that point, I had never even been to a gay nightclub!

Dan was perfect for me at this stage of my life. He took this almost country boy and allowed me to find different aspects of myself and bring them out to be polished. He showed me how to appreciate high-end restaurants and hotels; he transformed my dress sense and offered new ways to mature in my style; he even took me to his incredible hairdresser in Sydney, who ran this awesome little barbershop in one of the side streets of Surry Hills and used the C word so often she had it tattooed on her body. She got rid of my very heterosexual hairstyle (which included that small part at the back of your hair that spikes out a bit) and changed it up so I was a little more well-groomed.

We would spend our weekends wandering tree-lined streets filled with cafes and bookshops, exploring new exhibitions, meeting with friends for cool experiences like kayaking the coast, enjoying Sydney beaches, or trying new restaurants. We would work out in boot camps or at gyms in the morning and lie in parks on sunny afternoons, and one of my happiest memories is when we would go running around Hyde Park and Wolloomooloo on late Sunday afternoons, before flying back to Brisbane for work.

At this stage, I was still heavily involved in community projects in Brisbane outside of work, lived with Rachel and Sam, and would spend time with close friends and family on the weekends. He was close to his family, but as he lived away from them, he didn't see them as much. Given all the changes I was undergoing, in many ways, I felt like he enjoyed the energy and lifestyle I brought to the table. As fabulous as life can be in Sydney, it can be fickle, superficial, and overwhelming at times. I loved my weekends down there, as his friends were kind and inclusive, but I could imagine it would be tiring after a while. When we were in Brisbane, we would spend time with his sister and brother-in-law, who lived in Brisbane, and he would get to know my family too, including my gorgeous little niece who had just recently been born. I would take him to football matches and other events, where I am sure he felt we were all just a little bit "bogan." This always made me laugh, whether it was true or not.

When it came to relationships, I was realizing that there was a lot I didn't know about myself, let alone about this new community I was joining. I would learn about things I hadn't known before, but also see different types of insecurities or hurt that Dan was living with as a result of someone who had been part of the community for so many years. Whether we like it or not, the gay community has its own set of rules and expectations that have developed over time. Whether it is a result of having to create relationships under the watchful eye of prejudice and hate, or whether it is the reality of same-sex relationships, I began to see some liberating ideals, as much as I saw realities that seemed to be accepted despite the fact that it wasn't healthy for the individual.

I recall lying on the bed one day with him in his apartment that overlooked Darlinghurst, Potts Point, and Sydney Harbour. We were chatting about how I wouldn't see him for a week or so as he wasn't coming back to Brisbane for work. I felt myself feeling sad about this, but also feeling a little insecure leaving him, as I saw how he was surrounded by so much "opportunity." As I reflect back on this feeling, it was certainly a mixture of me projecting my own insecurities on the situation, as I had not experienced life as I should have, but I was also aware that for all I knew, he could have someone else chasing him, and in this fickle space, he may be just as tempted to go and find someone else who looked prettier or who offered more than I could. We could argue this feeling is common to all relationships, but I had seen how liberal everyone was about relationships and sex and it made me feel uneasy. For the first time, I was uncertain about whether I could trust him. Or maybe I was feeling uncertain about whether I could trust myself. I'm not sure.

I addressed this concern with him and his response was vague. It wasn't that he was saying anything wrong, but he wasn't saying anything that made me feel "safe" again. This uncertainty later translated to my own lack of integrity. I was learning that you just want to know you are safe in a relationship. If I was to pinpoint the moment our relationship changed, this would be it. I felt uncertain and had not been given anything but vagueness in return. As I was lacking in self-awareness about the whole situation, I allowed this vague approach to cloud my own judgment and did silly, reckless things, like continue to speak to Jake. I know it was bordering on poor behavior, but I felt like the boundaries had been blurred and maybe, as I had no ill intentions, it would be okay.

It was around April, when we had seen each other quite a lot and our relationship was growing, when he found the messages on my phone from

Jake. We had been chatting, and Jake was still adamant that we shouldn't let each other go. I allowed these messages to continue and put myself, and my integrity, into a compromising position. Including one that could hurt this new man in my life. Dan was heartbroken to find these messages, and it brought up a world of insecurities for him. Little did I know that the gay world is riddled with insecurities when it comes to relationships. I didn't understand why he was so hurt as our previous conversations seemed so vague and liberal about how the world of relationships could be, but I understood that he was hurt to think I could be so foolish. I stepped away from our relationship for a few days to get my head around it all. I, too, was hurt and had old feelings of loneliness and rejection come up again, not to mention confusion around what this new landscape looked like for me. With no certainty from Jake yet again, I decided that I had to let him go once and for all, and heal my pain of rejection. I decided that I would continue with this new relationship that was bringing me joy and growth. We had only been together a few months at this point, and it seemed like such a loss to break up and not explore more of the world with this man. As we were both in the airline world, Dan and I decided to go to Bali together, to get away for a few days and reconnect. This trip was not only fun and fabulous, it was healing. It allowed me to reconnect without any other distractions. It set us up for the remainder of our time in Australia together. I would go to Sydney most weekends, and he would come to Brisbane all week to work. We created a life between the two cities, which was quite fabulous in theory, and he slowly introduced me to more of the "gay world."

When we were in Sydney, I started to learn more about how my new community operates. I felt comically out of place at times, and would watch what was going on around me in an almost objective way. It was like a *National Geographic* piece: *The gays seem to flock together, always moving from one venue to another in groups. In social situations, they are like peacocks, shaking their colorful feathers and showing off to one another. They don't like messy nests, with only the best items being brought back to make their home shine. Although, the size of their home isn't so important, as long as they are in the center of where the action takes place. The gays are a fit bunch too, working tirelessly on their bodies to ensure that they attract only the best of their male counterparts.*

    I joke and digress, but it is hilarious to look back on. I recall similar memories, thinking how different life was down there, almost distant to the one I was leading in Brisbane. But I enjoyed the fun of it all. These were my new people, and I had to find out as much as I could to fit in.

The year went on, and we came to around July, when my next 'itch" took place. I had been on such a roller-coaster ride for a few years at that point, and was growing tired of this same old scene. Yes, I had a great boyfriend. Yes, I was settled into my job and doing well. Yes, I had a good network of friends. But I was teeming for more.

Similar to Virgin Australia, I was friends with the Head of Department for Etihad Airways, Gary, and their current staff travel manager. I saw that the manager was leaving the company, and immediately saw an opportunity to jump ship and find that next adventure. I sent Gary a Facebook message to ask about the job and let him know I would be perfect for the role. Within a few weeks I had a phone interview, followed by an offer. The process to move took longer, with the need for approvals and police clearances in the UAE holding us up. I told Dan about my job offer and that I was keen to take it if I got it. This rattled him. After all that we had been through in our relationship to this point—the ups and downs of our breakup and Jake, the trials and tribulations of creating a new life with someone—and now here I was looking to move overseas. Naturally, he wanted to retreat and cool things down between us. I didn't want that though, and made a point that we need to stay together until I officially leave, as it is just a waste of something special. We could decide at that point if we should break it off or see where to take it. While he was initially reluctant, he agreed.

With the thought that Dan and I were going to have to break up, time became even more precious between us. It created spark in the relationship that was lacking before, and I grew even more attached to him. We stayed together up until the day I left. It was so hard to say good-bye, not only to him but to everyone in my life, including those people whom I had met through him in Sydney and around Australia. At the same time though, I was excited about what lay ahead for me. I had been craving this change and opportunity to move back overseas for years, and now, finally feeling my whole self for the first time, the universe had planned for this change to happen. How could I not be grateful?

Thinking it was our goodbye, he sent me the most beautiful message, with a poem from a childhood favorite, Dr. Seuss, that still puts a smile on my face until today;

"If ever there is a tomorrow when we're not together... there is something you must always remember.

You are braver than you believe, stronger than you seem, and smarter than you think. But the most important thing is, even if we're apart, I'll always be with you."

It wasn't long before the universe decided to test me a little further and see if I was ready to be on my own or not. Dan came to visit the UAE a month or so later for his birthday, a trip which I was looking forward to as we were still missing one another. While he was in town, we were chatting with a friend of mine who was the head of HR for Etihad. He couldn't understand why Dan wasn't here as well, so he put him in touch with the teams locally for a chat. Before we knew it, he was offered a job at Etihad as well!

Without thinking about it too much, we decided that since we were still together (despite the distance), we should move in with one another. It made sense financially, after all! At the time, I was so caught up in wanting to make this relationship work, that I didn't really consider what I was feeling deep down. If I am honest with myself now, I would say a large part of me—and I am sure of him too—was thinking maybe we shouldn't move in together. But another big part of me was lonely, missed him terribly, and could see me managing a relationship well in our new home. This is where I was using what I knew around me to set expectations for what I "thought" I wanted, and where I forced it to happen. I used to see Rachel and Sam and think how I want to find that type of love. I wanted to be with someone who made me that happy and who I could build a life together with. I was also only twenty-five, had only come into my new skin a year ago, and was now living overseas. But none of that crosses your mind, you just think about what you "should" be creating. So not listening to my gut or the universe, I went ahead with the plan and began creating a home with him in January.

Despite where this led, creating a place together and living out this ideal I had in my mind was fun to begin with. It was superficial, given it was in such dissonance with how I really felt, but I pushed forward and we kept filling our space and time with lots of things. The new space was short-lived and by around August that year, we decided to break up. How did we go from creating a home in January to being split up by August? Well, that is the reality of not living authentically. As I can only speak for myself, throughout that year we created a lifestyle that wasn't sustainable, our communication was poor and riddled with emotional blocks, and we were not on the same page when it came to our sex life. I was not accepting the fact that I felt deep down that I had not yet explored the world. Dan had been out for most of his life, and so his relationships until this point were authentic to his own self. I was brand-new to it all! I would find myself in nightclubs or in cities around the world, as we traveled together quite a bit, and feeling desires to want to meet other people or explore things sexually. Yet, despite his vague approach on relationships, he wouldn't want to do anything out of the norm when it came to our sex life. It was as if he wanted a monogamous relationship, which is fine, but didn't always make me feel like he wanted to be in it. This isn't about him though, but rather about the fact that I never cleared this up or allowed enough self-awareness to see this at the time, as I was so lost and caught up in my own dissonance between how I felt and what I was creating.

When I look back over this year, it was another significant year of growth, but it was also a year of challenging my own integrity. I began to be reckless and, in the end, we would have arguments more than we would be kind and loving to one another. I remember one night, which was a moment I am in no way proud of, and haven't really spoken about before, I allowed the blurred lines to be used to expose how I was feeling. I couldn't seem to find my own capacity to address my feelings and talk about them, so I allowed poor behavior to show it. We were lying in bed and I was feeling so distant and upset with our relationship. I think we had had an argument and I couldn't sleep. I got my phone out and I downloaded Scruff—a gay hookup app—that I still had access to from when I was single. I started scrolling through online, wondering if I was missing out on something more in the world and who was around me in this new city. Aware that I was running a huge risk, but slightly unaware that he could see my phone, Dan rolled over and caught me. "Are you on Scruff?" he exclaimed. I felt myself freeze, like a child caught with his hand in the lolly jar, and became suddenly so aware of what I was doing, why I was doing it, and how wrong it was. I closed my phone, feeling shocked at myself, the reality I was creating, and how embarrassed I felt—while feeling somewhat relieved to be caught. He jumped out of bed, understandably furious, and stormed out of the room. What had I done? This was the beginning of the end.

Even telling this story brings up memories of shame for me, but it is important to share it. Because for so many people, we live in this space of dissonance and deceit. In our evolving technological era, I have met so many people while I was single who are actively in a relationship but living like this, with no regard for what they are doing to themself and the other person involved, and it breaks my heart. I did such a stupid act because I was feeling lost, unloved, unheard, unseen, and mostly, unsafe. I wasn't receiving what I needed to know that I was safe and open to explore myself within the boundaries of this relationship. And in many ways, that was a good thing, because I needed to go and do that on my own. But, as a result of this, I acted in ways that were not reflective of my true self and of the person I wanted to become. It was showing the dark, sad, and unresolved side of me that wasn't strong enough to just say "enough." At the end of the day though, I am only human, as we all are, and some of our connections are designed to challenge us and help us grow. This relationship was my first real relationship, in my new skin. And this situation was my first time living with a partner. I should have listened to myself from the very beginning, but I kept pushing a forced expectation of what life should look like and this was the result. Looking back on it, I know that I was right for Dan at the time, as much as he was for me at the time. But in the same breath, we both needed someone who didn't quite fit what we offered each other. Instead of growing together, we, unfortunately, grew apart. And in the end, it broke us.

At the time, it felt like the biggest disappointment, and I was guilt-riddled. I felt like I could have done more; I felt like I deserved more. I felt like I was not a good enough person, as I had certainly made some poor decisions along the way. The list went on. But most of all, I knew that he deserved someone who could give him what it was he was looking for. And that wasn't me. I believed so even after another year, post breakup, of still sleeping together and continuing on those horrendous "what if" conversations about getting back together. Those destructive, soul-destroying conversations allow situations to linger far beyond the time frame they were once destined for, and into a place where both parties start to show their worst selves. It was so stupid of us to let our connection get tainted, but again, at the time you know nothing else. We have all been there! No matter who I speak to, we all have an example of this time in a relationship that has finished. Why don't we just find a way to stop? Why don't we accept that we are sailing into the wind of the universe and our boat is getting battered? Why don't we trust the lessons learned and allow ourselves to move forward?

This relationship taught me ***the importance of integrity***. Integrity for me is the space between how people perceive you and your genuine intentions. When this space gets too large, it means that you are off course. It indicates that while your intentions may be correct to you, they may not be true to those around you. Maybe you have something in your mind that you want from life, but you are pushing against it to ensure that those around you get what they want, only to find that you are creating an even wider space between that reality and your own. A divide between your ideal self and the self that people see. We do this in relationships too. And when I was in the most complicated parts of this relationship was when my authentic intentions (that feeling that lingered deep in my gut) did not align with how people perceived me.

We all do this in our own right at times, as we battle with what we think we want, what the universe wants, and what we think other people need. And whether it hurts some people around you, or changes your situation, you have to stay true to yourself and your integrity. If you feel like you shouldn't be in that particular relationship, don't start showing behaviors that may question your values. Own that your feelings have changed, forget the fear of scarcity, and go with your intentions. If those intentions see you elsewhere, own it. Sometimes I wish I dared to have done that earlier. But, I am not one to question the lessons in the universe, and I think that while that would have seen me move on quicker, it would have missed some other crucial life lessons along the way.

A VISIONARY AT WORK

During my time with Dan, I found myself living and working in Abu Dhabi. It was always a dream for me to be back overseas, and after nearly five years of hard work at Virgin, lots of amazing experiences, coming to terms with more of my authentic self, welcoming my first niece into the world, and beginning my "first real relationship" with Dan, that 'itch" sparked again. One afternoon after work, as I was walking to my car, I checked my Facebook and saw an update by an acquaintance I had met through work in Abu Dhabi. He was the manager of the staff travel team for Etihad, the national carrier of the UAE, and after a year in the role decided it was time to head home. While I am sure it would be sad to see him go, the entrepreneur inside immediately saw an opportunity. I messaged his boss, who happened to be a friend of mine, to ask about the role and tell him of my interest. In no time, I had a phone interview with him and HR to discuss the opportunity. A few weeks later, the offer came through. I thought I was Willy Wonka and had just received my golden ticket, in more ways than one! The process took a few months as I began my first lessons of life in that part of the world, but before I knew it, it was time to go.

Ever since I returned from working in London, I kept looking for a new way to get overseas again and make the most of my work life. I knew I had to get away from Australia, not because life was terrible or anything—by no means did I have even a difficult life in the slightest. I had a deep desire to be living my life abroad. I had dreamt about it from when I was twenty and I would write passages in my journal about the life I would live. I would write about everything down to the type of wardrobe I would create for myself that reflected the person I would be. Actually, there were two wardrobes; one filled with really nice suits and corporate wear, and the other, a cool, casual collection of outfits that allowed for my life of travel, socializing, and fitness. I never quite understood it, but I knew it had to happen at some point. All of a sudden, I was at the airport, family and boyfriend by my side, tears flowing, but a quiet excitement stirring inside of me.

For the first six months in Abu Dhabi, it was entirely up and down, as expected. I was in a new position, where on my first day in the office my boss wasn't there. I was fumbling through with what suddenly felt like minimal knowledge, and in so many new situations defined by cultures I had never spent time with before. These situations found me meeting with my team where Indian and Sri Lankan culture dictated work methods. It saw me working in an aggressive work culture where "winning" was celebrated from the top down, and fear was rife. On weekends, I would find myself with people from backgrounds and cultures that I have never spent time with, and in places that made Dorothy feel like she wasn't in Kansas anymore! It was like I had stepped into a time machine or into some altered reality that my own vision board or journal had the capacity to write about ahead of this time.

The work was challenging, not by a lack of knowledge, but by sheer volume and speed of its requirement. The department had a terrible reputation, filled with ancient processes and poor leadership. Management was existent, but there is a huge difference between managing people and leading them. I had to be firmer and more direct than I had been before and deal with impatient and demanding upper management (thankfully, my immediate boss excluded). I had to learn to play a very aggressive corporate game of always being "right," and most of all, maintaining my composure the whole time, while still being a strong and empathetic leader. I spent a large portion of my time stressed, anxious, high-strung, and angry—albeit on the inside for the most part. The experience of working in this environment was overwhelming, demanding, and nonstop. I would get home after a twelve-hour day at work, be climbing into bed, and my Blackberry would ring with someone requiring after-hours support (which had not previously been outlined in the job description!). I didn't mind doing this work as it fed into the identity I thought I was creating for myself, but it didn't allow any time for me to be calm. Every time I looked at my phone, a new request was coming through, a new problem needed to be solved, or a new drama had been created. Every time I walked into the office I would be attacked by people who constantly wanted something from me. At the time, it was confronting, but over time I became used to it and I think it got worse. When we start normalizing such crazy behavior, we should start to worry. Cross-fit during the weeks was great for coping, and drinking on the weekend was my other "go-to" to help with the stress. Not that it helped at all with my overall well-being! And my new network of friends was making a huge difference in my world.

What I established very quickly in this job was that if I wanted to succeed, I would require a strong and clear vision. I learned that I didn't have someone else deciding this vision for me, it was up to me to make it happen and ensure that everyone was on board. And once I had a clear idea of what I wanted our department to look like, it didn't mean it was smooth sailing either. Nope. Every day I had to work my ass off to ensure that everyone on my team worked toward the same outcome, every department understood what we were working toward, and that I had the full support of those above me to achieve this. It was bold, and it had to be resilient, especially within that environment.

Over the following years, work became more manageable, and with this vision and perseverance, I grew and progressed the department toward my desired success. In fact, after only a couple of years, we had some fantastic wins, like increasing the team from twelve people across three locations to sixty-plus people across six sites, including overseeing airport operations (which was a significant issue when I first arrived, and well outside of my original remit of work). Our reputation had improved significantly, service excelled, and I had managed to create a team of highly skilled agents and leaders who not only could handle our customers better than before, but they enjoyed coming to work. I am sure I wasn't a perfect leader at times, but it was as if the universe was testing everything I had learned up until that point to prove to me that I was capable of achieving my goals in the business world.

This experience saw me grow both on a personal and professional front; it saw me utilize my skills to develop other people, influence company culture, and implement real benefits for employees. It also taught me the power of resilience. Some days, I would be knocked down over and over again, and yet, I had to get back up. I had to be resilient to the knocks if I wanted to achieve my vision. For me, this was one of the biggest lessons in my work life to date. In all that we do, in all that we want to achieve, the difference between those that make it and those that do not is resilience. To be resilient means staying true to what your core values are. Resilience doesn't mean that we have to take a beating for the sake of it. Instead, take a knockdown, stand back up, and get on with the work. A bold vision is what will drive the work, but the resilience of the leader is what will bring it to life.

At the same time as I was achieving my goal from a business perspective, I was also impacting my life from a spiritual perspective. I had taken this hard-and-fast life for granted, and I was living it in every aspect of myself. I would wake by 7:00 each morning, work until 6:30, Cross-fit each night, then go from training to dinner either at a friend's or out at a restaurant, then home by 10:30-11:00, to either sleep or possibly have a 'friend' over. This was my life for quite a while (once I was single of course, after Dan and I broke up). And on the weekends, I would normally meet friends and go out Thursday night, beach or pool day Friday, go out Friday night, and spend Saturday recovering. Again, usually with some random hookups in between. Throw into the mix of this a high-stress job occupying my time, extra work tasks on the weekends (despite usually being intoxicated or out), and random trips away each month to some destination around the world so I could party and have fun—it makes for a life filled with heavy impact and no solace or respite. As expected, in between this I would usually get sick a few times throughout the year, when my tired body couldn't take any more of the antics. And whilst this may sound like fun to some people, and at the time it felt like it was to me, I also didn't allow myself any time to know any different. I worked myself into such a frenzy that this routine permeated my state of being and created the person I was by the end of this job. Agitated, anxious, highly strung, and selfish. My compassion and empathy levels were low, I was happy to use people (as I felt like they continued to use me), I pushed for whatever I felt I wanted and beat myself up when it didn't happen. On the outside, I was a happy-go-lucky person, but beneath that exterior, I felt angry, lost, and fed up. My soul was undernourished and my reality had become everything I had asked for. The "itch" for something better was lost in a sea of materialistic obsession and days filled with completing tasks I no longer believed in.

I had great achievements in this role and I proved to myself everything I was capable of delivering up until that point. But by my last year with the company, I was tired, jaded, and seeking the day-light of opportunity, where I felt like the darkness of night surrounded me. I didn't know how I would possibly move out of this space, and even if I did, I was not inspired by the ideas that my limited mind could come up with.

It was a shame that I was in such a space as it took me some time after this period to look back and realize the power of my lesson, which was **The Power of a Clear Vision**. When I stepped off that plane in Abu Dhabi to begin this role, I had a clear vision of what I wanted to achieve. I had no idea what lay ahead, and I am certain I probably would have run away from the opportunity if I had known half of what I was about to be dealt. But had I not had that clear vision to implement the service structures, processes, and deliverables that I knew I was capable of delivering, it would have been really hard to get started, or impossible to achieve. A clear vision isn't just about knowing where you are steering the ship, it's about feeling every part of the success in your body; physically, emotionally, even spiritually before it is manifested in reality. Despite how tired, lost, and jaded I felt, I managed to achieve exactly what I set out to do. I didn't do it alone, but with the support of an incredible team of people who were committed to delivering that vision.

THE CHAMPION

25 March, 2016. This day will remain one of the most memorable dates of my life. It was the day I met my "champion." For the last six months before meeting this man, something had shifted in the way I saw the world. I suddenly became aware of the life I had created in Abu Dhabi. The nonstop, soulless existence I was living. I started to grow tired of my promiscuous and reckless ways. I felt lonelier than ever, despite being surrounded by people all the time, and I felt like there had to be more to life. I craved balance, but I had no idea how I could find it. My behavior, my attitude, and my lifestyle dictated my reality, and I had minimal self-control when it came to "slowing down." But, amongst this chaos, I felt a quiet "itch" showing itself. A feeling that I craved for more than what I had. One that was quietly asking me to calm my world, so that I wouldn't miss seeing what was about to arrive.

At the time, I was seeing a Jordanian guy. Well, we saw each other, but I was far from committed, which is sad because he was a great guy—handsome, kind, and loving. Albeit, he wasn't "out" yet, so that for me put an immediate stop to anything ever eventuating. Irrelevant of how crazy I may have been at the time, I wasn't stupid in knowing that if I did end up with someone, they at least had to own who they rightfully were. I had been through that cycle, and I know it isn't a great place to be either personally or in relationships. As I started to slow down on the chaos, I began mentioning to friends that I wouldn't mind being in a relationship. I wasn't sure what it looked like and who this guy would be, but I felt like it is what I wanted. In fact, I said that I was going to own being single, because "I want a champion, and he will come and stop me in my tracks." I think by this point people thought I was either utterly mental or conceited. One friend was quite annoyed at this comment, as she felt that I couldn't have the best of both worlds—freely single and then demand a so-called champion to appear. For some reason though, I seemed to disagree.

I didn't have an articulated version of who this guy would be, but I had a feeling. Only with hindsight can I start to see the traits and qualities I was craving. It may seem high level, but I wanted someone who was going to not only make me feel wanted, but make me feel safe and secure. I wanted to feel loved without condition. I wanted stimulation intellectually and spiritually. I wanted someone who had a great relationship with their family. I wanted someone who was comfortable enough with themselves that they could help me work through my issues. I wanted someone who was driven and successful in their field of work. I wanted someone creative and with some flair. I wanted personality, but I also wanted them to be soft when it came to our emotions. I was hard enough as it was; the last thing I needed was another hardball. At the same time, I knew I needed someone who would also be firm with me when I needed it. This last idea I couldn't say was a "want," as I had become accustomed to getting my way with men, but I knew I needed it for growth.

I wanted someone with a different cultural background, but I also wanted some level of familiarity. And I wanted passion. I was so tired of meeting people who were just drifting through life. I found myself craving someone with passion and energy. I had it in me, why couldn't they have it too?

I didn't sit and write down all of these wants and needs at the time. As I look back, I feel like I should have, as it would have made it easier to know what I was looking for, rather than just handing it to the universe and saying "please deliver." But, what I did ask for was a champion who would knock me off my feet. And, well, without being able to articulate these feelings, but to have them thrown in front of me with this new guy, certainly gave me what I asked for. I was knocked to the ground, really quickly.

Toward the end of 2015, I had a friend request pop up on Facebook for a guy whom I had seen around on social media through mutual friends, but whom I had never met in person. *That was weird*, I thought. *I haven't even met this guy, why is he adding me?* So I left it. Little did I know, he was going through his own roller coaster of change at the time. After a few months, I mentioned to friends about it, to see who this guy was. I would even go back and just look at his picture—he seemed so familiar, but I couldn't figure out why. He had a handsome face, shaped beard, and he looked like he had some ethnic background, but I couldn't figure what it was. I would have said Arab, given where we lived, but I had learned that you just never know. He had lovely eyes. Almond. Deep. Almost piercing. My first thought was, "Did I sleep with him before?" But nothing came to mind. He intrigued me, but something kept saying "not now."

By March 2016, before I was home for my birthday, I gave in and decided that I would add him back on Facebook. I looked for his profile—Bryan—and I accepted him. We started chatting, trying to piece together if we had met. I don't even recall the chat, but I know it was good. He was slightly mysterious, but funny and witty all at the same time. I love a bit of sarcasm, and he seemed to know this well. We decided after chatting a couple of times that the banter was good enough for a date and agreed to have dinner when I was back in Abu Dhabi. The planning began, and it took a couple of weeks before we made it happen. It seemed our mutual acquaintances had other ideas for our meeting and started to offer advice that would seem to deter us from going on a date. Based on the wonderful advice of these people, I was deemed to be the type of guy that would "use people" and was only looking for a good time—a reputation that, based on my actions, I couldn't really argue with. It was never my intention to use anyone during my lost years on Grindr, but given my crazy promiscuity, I was not surprised. It was hard to hear these things, especially from a guy I was about to go on a date with, when I knew that the person that people were perceiving—irrelevant of whether they have a wholesome reputation to stand by or not—was not the person I was at heart.

In the end, we decided that we were adults and that meeting was inevitable—so why not make a fabulous night of it? We would meet at a Lebanese restaurant in the Rosewood. This choice wouldn't have been my first, but I learned over time from Bryan after learning about his heritage, that in Persian culture, you never go back to the place where you first met. With this in mind, I could see why this wouldn't be an issue. On March 25th, we met at 7:00 pm at the Rosewood. I was early, surprise, and so waited on the lounge on the terrace of the restaurant, by the fire. It was a chilly evening still this time of year. Friends of mine, Casey and Craig, were downstairs at Zuma having dinner, and were on standby for "emergency SOS" should the evening turn out to be dire.

When he walked in, it was an odd feeling. I looked up and saw this man of average height—which was shorter than I expected—a thick build, shaved head, beard, and the same lovely almond eyes I had seen online, come walking toward me. I sat next to a fire pit on the balcony of the restaurant, overlooking the city. The surrounding lights and the glow from the fire lit him up as he walked over. He spotted me and came over to where I was sitting. He smiled and shook my hand. He was late, which was expected in this region, but I, for once, had been on time. He apologized and asked if we should go straight to our table. I was adamant that this would be a disaster, as other dates before had been, so I was somewhat cautious around him. I was waiting for the barrage of conversation where he'd tell me all about him, what he did, who he was, and why he was so wonderful, with little thought to ask much about me. I thought that as long as he could hold a decent conversation, we might get a nice night and a shag out of it, because let's be honest, love is hard to find in this city.

When I think back to those initial moments, I think about the idea of "love at first sight." Some people talk about it and society seems to have a connection with "love" in that it feels all light, fluffy, and romantic. But for me, this moment wasn't the same as the others. He was someone who I hadn't met before, yet he looked so familiar. It was an intense moment like I was meeting an old friend from a long time ago, and it was just that awkward moment before you begin to reminisce and allow the memories to reconnect you. The only way I could describe the moment I met him is that he reminded me of the same familiarity that I have when I see my family. And for someone who was lost, scattered, and expecting to have dinner and shag at most, it completely caught me off guard. I couldn't call it at this point, but it wasn't until a year in that I realized he was the image of the person that my "all-consuming love" represented. I mentioned earlier that when I met Jake, he felt so familiar. Well, all I could say is this must have been it.

We sat down, and the banter began. I could tell he was nervous. He told me he was. We kicked off with the usual chitchat, trying to build on our phone conversations, but we were both a little unsure. To break the ice, he said that he had written a list of questions we could ask each other if we got stuck. I thought he was joking and I laughed. He laughed too, but then he showed me that he really did have a list on his phone. I laughed some more. "Ok then," I said, "hit me with some of your questions." Initially I thought, *No matter how awkward we think this could be, there is no way that I cannot hold a conversation with you without the need for some silly question list.* But his list was good and the questions kicked off a night of nonstop conversation. We spoke about everything—from our first love to open relationships; dreams and aspirations to our most significant fears; political views and spiritual ideals. The night rushed past, and seven hours later when we sat at the bar downstairs in Zuma, it was 2:00 am, the lights came up, and we had to call it a night. Given my recent "dating" experiences, I expected that he would want to come home or see where else we could take this. Instead, like a real gentleman, he called me a cab outside, kissed me on the cheek, and we said good night. I was rattled. How could I have had such a fabulous night, such great banter, have it last for seven hours, and now be sent on my way with a kiss? I didn't think people like this existed? Who was this guy? And why was I so shocked to be treated so respectfully? What does it say about me, when he extends courtesy like this, and I am questioning it? During the evening, we had discussed the realities of what it means to be seeing someone new and the games that usually entails. I told him that I don't do games when I like someone, and if you decide to play games, you will just miss out. In the cab on the way home, with this conversation in mind, I pushed myself without any hesitation into the ultimate place of vulnerability—I messaged him immediately. I told him how much of an incredible night I had, reminded him not to play games with me, and told him to message me if he felt like it, and that I couldn't wait to do it again. He politely replied, which was a relief, considering my vulnerable state, and we called it a night. The next day, I hadn't heard from him at all. I was still rattled. I felt like something big had been shifted inside of me. I wanted more. Not in the usual way of just having sex, but I wanted to know more, talk more, explore more. I was genuinely interested. By 4:00 pm, I hadn't received a message, and I knew he was playing it cool. So, like I am sure a stalker could look, I messaged him first, "Are you alive?" Nice. Real subtle, Luke. That was the last of the "playing it cool" games from his side. The following weekend we met again, and again he sent me home with a kiss. The next time we met, which was at my house, I cornered him on the couch and said he has one chance left to at least kiss me properly. Otherwise, he was going to be in the express lane to the friend zone. Luckily, that was all he needed to hear before the gentleman was pushed aside for a minute.

It is now two years on from when we first met, as I write this book, and I have to say that we are even more connected and in love than we were the first day we met. Each day, we only seem to get stronger and more aligned. I don't mean this in a fairy-tale sense, but one built on growth, discovery, kindness, support, and most importantly, love. Vulnerable, unconditional, nonjudgmental, uncompromising, love. A type of love that comes with all the same challenges that each of us experience, but one where, no matter how large the hurdle, there is only one way for every solution—and that is, how can we respectfully resolve this with both of our best interests in mind?

Don't get me wrong, though. We have had some fallings-out along the way, and it has found me internally challenged at times not to fall back into my old ways of thinking. In the first four to six months, I was waiting for this to all be "too good to be true" and have him walk out on me. To the point that, even in the first few months, I found potential distractions still showing up that would have sabotaged the whole relationship. The difference this time was that I could feel that there was something more here. Whether it was old flings still trying to contact me or taking some pre-planned overseas trips with friends with whom I had a history, the universe was testing me. It was also starting me off on the long and arduous journey of cleaning out the closet and saying good-bye to old, toxic relationships that I had allowed to linger for too long. It was hard at the beginning, as I had just met this guy and wasn't even sure if he would turn out to be a joke in the end—all smoke and mirrors. But somehow, I could see the benefits of trusting in my gut and remaining vulnerable with him. At this stage, what did I have to lose by trusting in one person rather than flaunting myself around the place? If I believed I would be happier ruining this and going back to my old life, I am sure I would have done it. But I loved this guy and was intrigued and excited and learning, every day. I think that had me the most. I could feel myself growing and learning with him. We challenged each other. We argued. We debated. We agreed and celebrated. For the first time, I realized what it felt like to want to show up for a relationship in a healthy and balanced way. But it required me, every day, to do exactly that. Consciously show up and decide to be there. Too often we think we need something else or something more, when it is our fear of being vulnerable that stops us from rolling over and just giving one more kiss, or stopping them and telling them that you love them; or sharing that you feel hurt and upset by an action which you need to remedy.

In our relationship, Bryan has taught me things about myself that no one has ever shown me. Everything from self-worth and personal value, to spirituality and service. Even if he wasn't "teaching me" about it himself, his love and support offered me the space to be able to find it for myself. This is in the same way that the young Luke, before coming out, would go into his bedroom each night to read books and write about his dreams. And this love and support I have equally offered back to him. Together, we have both grown significantly as individuals—we have opened our own company together called Blonde and Bear—a business concept design service that assists individuals and entrepreneurs with bringing their ideas to life; we have created businesses for other people—up to fifty brands and business concepts to date. We have worked with friends and family on finding their purpose and, in between, we have been lucky enough to travel the world. Throughout that time we have learned what love means to us as a couple, and to each other individually, what our sexual needs require, where we draw the lines in our relationship without compromising on what brings us joy and connection, and even what joy looks like to us both. And the best part of all of this is that we have actively done it without any societal frameworks pushing us toward a predetermined place in life. We have chosen to do it out of love for one another and with a desire to be the best versions of ourselves.

So why has this relationship been the most successful for me so far? Because we have both actively chosen to be in it; to offer kindness, support, and love; to not compromise on what matters most to each of us; and to offer each other open and honest communication. The last two points, I believe, have also been integral to making this work. To not compromise, does not mean to be stubborn or rigid. It means to listen to what the other person wants to do and actively decide on whether that suits your needs or not. If you do not mind, then you do it out of love for that person. If it is something that does not suit you, then you be honest and share your views. This discussion doesn't mean that it won't happen, but the point is that by sharing your thoughts, you will be able to discuss the matter and decide on what to do next. That is where communication comes into it. To communicate isn't just to speak or offer words of advice, it is mostly to listen and ensure that each person can be heard without judgment.

So far, this relationship has taught me more lessons that I can include in this book. Some were reiterated from past experiences, and others have been brand-new for me. I have learned about the importance of ensuring all the fundamentals of any relationship are always present—like respect, kindness, open communication, no need to compromise, and unconditional love. This is what has made our relationship so unique to this point, and in my opinion what will be our anchor to remain together for whatever time we are meant to be.

But one key lesson that I have learned and that continues is that in any relationship, **every day you have a choice to actively show up.** Every day it is so imperative that we wake up and consciously choose to actively be in that relationship. Whether it takes you a moment to acknowledge or some self-work to reconnect with your space, it is required to truly make something of a relationship. Ideally, this connection will give you gratitude for what you have, as relationships can be hard work at times. They show you sides of yourself and your partner that you wouldn't always choose to see. It demands of you more empathy, love, and understanding than you may be willing to offer some days. You have to choose not to self-sabotage when you feel like it is getting difficult. And you have to lean into that vulnerable feeling. I know, for many people, that the thought of vulnerability means weakness or opening yourself to get hurt. But guess what, no matter what you do in life, you can always get hurt! So, you might as well lean into it and enjoy it for what it is. For all you know, that may be for the rest of your life. And if it isn't, at least you know at the end of that relationship, that you gave it all you could. You gave every bit of love, care, attention, kindness, and support you could. You provided an opportunity for that person you love to grow and for your soul to evolve. And, if it was to end, you lost nothing at all, as the time invested was well spent.

Every day it is up to each of us to make our relationships a reflection of who we are. It is up to us to create our love stories and allow that love to blossom. And it is up to each of us to consciously choose to share our lives with that special person. I know I do. Every day, I choose my actions and reactions, I choose to offer myself in love as much as I can, and I choose to be the man that my champion deserves and that I deserve to be. I actively choose to show up for my relationship and at times, it has been one of the toughest and most rewarding lessons I have learned in love so far. Because no matter what happens, I know every day I chose to be there.

And I can safely add that to this day, no matter the outcome, he remains, and will always remain, "my champion."

SERVING IN A GLOBAL COMMUNITY

In between 2010 and 2016, I visited Nepal a handful of times, each time bringing someone new, catching up with old friends and revisiting one or two of the villages to see our families and if our projects were still intact. In 2016, I decided to take my partner, Bryan, along with me to Nepal, as I had shared so many of my stories with him. We spoke with Sanjaya on the lead up to the trip and arranged to be part of an existing project that was under way in a village, not far from the second village where I lived for a couple of months in 2009. This would give us an opportunity to provide some money for work that has to be completed, assist in doing the manual labor ourselves, and visit my homestay family in the village.

Sanjaya, as always, was kind and generous with offering to arrange this and find a place for us to stay. He had discovered the project through a friend of his, who had family in a village close by. The project was to finish a recently built Red Cross building that required painting, carpets, and furnishings. We decided to fund this ourselves and head over for a couple of days to assist with painting the building. I found it amusing, as I wasn't sure how Bryan would cope with this type of work. As an interior designer by trade, he is used to the work site, but maybe not so used to the actual work being done by him. Luckily enough he shone through and showed me how wrong I was!

When we arrived in Kathmandu, we spent a night in a hotel in the city. This allowed me time to show Bryan some of Thamel, one of the main tourist districts in the city, and get acquainted with this vast urban community. Sanjaya collected us the next morning and took us to the village. We met his friend, Bishnu, along the way, whose family generously allowed us to stay with them. It was his brother's family who were so kind to have us. Once we arrived in the village, we met everyone, did the customary Dal Bhat for mid-morning breakfast—rice and dal, usually served with spicy vegetable curry and some pickles—and headed off to the work site. In this time, we also met Sudip, the nephew of Bishnu, who was twenty-two years old and had a pretty good command of English. Phew! This will make things easier, we thought.

On the second day of work, we decided to finish up early so we could head over to the other village where my homestay family from a previous trip lived. I was super excited to get there and for Bryan to meet these people I spoke about for so long. As much as I wanted to arrive and finally tell Mum and Laxmi, who was like my own Nepalese mother, that I had finally met someone, I chose not to as I didn't think it was kind to start waving the flag in a community of people who were maybe a little culturally limited in their own views. This isn't to say it is something I hid on purpose, but it would not add value to our relationship if I had started talking about my sexual preferences. It was irrelevant, so he was introduced as yet another friend. In true Nepalese form, Sudip and his friend drove us to the village in the local ambulance. It was the only vehicle available apparently that we could "hitch" a ride in. The one thing you learn about this country is that it is always full of unexpected and random events.

When we arrived at the village, we made our way toward the house. I remembered the path, so made pace up the hill, which was quite steep. As we were halfway up, I heard Sanjaya call out to say to come back down. I had passed the house. *No I haven't*, I thought. *It is at the top of the hill.* Little did I know, they had in fact moved, but not by choice. Their house, which was a beautiful big traditional Nepalese house at the top of the hill, had been reduced to rubble as a result of the tragic earthquakes they experienced a year or so before. I was in shock. I had asked Sanjaya if the family was ok, to which he said they were. But I guess I wasn't specific enough to then ask if their property had been damaged too. When we arrived, Mum, Dad and their youngest girl, Pramila, were there to greet us. Mum was so excited to see me, which was such a lovely feeling. She made me immediately come in, sit down, and assessed how I look. The wonderfully honest approach to life that the Nepalese take can be confronting if you don't expect it. It's usually either a "you look fat" or "you are too much skinny." There isn't much in between that, other than a look and slight head movement to acknowledge you. The following questions usually cover where you are living, if you are married, why you aren't married (with continued confusion), and how is your family.

After that, it can be tough going, but you always make the most of it.

Here I was now, two years on from my last visit, sitting with this family who once took me into their beautiful big home, and now we were sheltered under a very hot iron roof. Their old house, which was a two-level traditional home made of local materials like wood, mud, and clay, was still in rubble, and the makeshift property consisted of a hard steel iron roof being held up, almost like a tent, against some very young, termite-infested wood that they had collected from the forest behind them. Some more tin covered the sides of the sitting area and one of the sleeping areas. They were exposed to the world and would have felt the very ends of each season with the materials making it extremely hot in summer and extremely cold in winter. The traditional house had two stories, so the kitchen and living area were downstairs and the beds were upstairs. The heat of the fire in the kitchen would keep a warm house during winter, as would the walls made of clay, wood, and other plant-based materials.

During our stay we sat and ate dal baht—Mum always made great food—drank some chai (tea) and spoke about the world with the help of our now-trusted translator, Sudip. We reminisced about times passed and talked about current issues and affairs, including the lack of support for rebuilding they were receiving from the Nepalese government. Understandably, they were struggling to get funding to restore their home, as Nepal's government has always seemed to fall short with supporting its people, and the country was still very much in a developing state.

Before it was time to go, the dad asked me about Facebook. Of course I had Facebook, I thought. He then proceeded to tell me he was on there, as was his son, Prakash, and that we should connect to stay in touch. I don't know what it is about the romanticized notion of visiting the village and stepping away from the world, but I recall initially the hardest part about leaving this family was that I didn't know how we would stay in touch, or if I would make it back again. I remember having tears in the car as we drove off because I had not a clue if that was the last time I would ever see them. Now, here we were exchanging Facebook accounts so we could connect in the virtual world, and it was throwing me off. I may be part of the younger generation, but something about this just seemed bizarre. This family is sitting here with barely a roof over their head, yet they have a phone and Facebook. I wonder what they see on there when they are relaxing at home at night, and how their perception of the world had changed from when I first met them, until now.

It's crazy. But, to be honest, it was also amazing, as I suddenly had that new age feeling of being OK to leave as I am now always connected with them.

As we wrapped up our visit, we shared our good-byes and made our way to the other side of the village, where our transport was waiting. We stopped past for the obligatory chat with the chief of the village and his family, and I took Bryan through the projects we had finished around the school and library. It was great to see them all still standing so many years on. As we began to leave, my mind was busy with ideas and my stomach churning with a sense of service. It felt wrong leaving this village, knowing that a family who once shared their home with me was now living in such despair. We spoke about what their plans were to rebuild, and the government was offering 3,000,000 rupees to each family to rebuild (about $3,000 USD), but this, too, was not enough. As a result of the earthquake, they had released a new building standard, which meant that they had to meet these criteria and get approval from the new authority (another way to funnel funding to more of their mates). While the idea logically makes sense, despite the apparent favors that were taking place, it meant that most homes would exceed this $3,000 USD budget. As the family, like many people in rural Nepal, live off their crops, sell a small amount of milk that their cows produce through the local co-op, and sell eggs in a recent business Dad started, it's clear to say that their income stream wasn't that high. They were discussing getting a loan, but I could only imagine how long that would take to fund and pay back. They did say that if they take the loan, hopefully, the government will give more funding which will clear this, but at this stage, that was just rumor. I was panicked just hearing the decisions being made about loans of this amount knowing how little they had. It was all a recipe for disaster. As we got back into the car, I sat in the back and looked forward at the rear of the driver's chair. *We can't leave like this without a plan*, I thought. I called for Bryan, who was behind me, and didn't even turn to look at him. "Are you thinking what I am thinking?" I ask. "Yep," he replied. And the decision was made—we would build their new home.

We had almost returned to the village we were staying in, when Bryan, who was overwhelmed by the experience, decided that we had to stop and walk the rest of the way. All four of us piled out of the car and started walking along the dirt road through the villages that led toward home. He was rattled and upset. I forgot how much this reality could hurt someone, especially someone like him, who is very spiritually aware and could seem to feel a lot more of what was happening than what most people would. We decided to clear our minds and start chatting to Sudip, as we walked, about what his plans were for the future. He had left college and went to pursue a range of different careers—many of which he was hesitant about, as he did want to leave the village, but also enjoyed being close to his family. Unfortunately for him, he found a few different opportunities over the years, of which all fell short, or he was scammed on. One of the prospects had him pay for chef training, only to find that the person arranging it ran off with his money. He was heartbroken from the experiences, lost, and seeking direction, but wasn't sure where to look. He loved the work that his Uncle Bishnu did with Sanjaya (the connection we had to meet him), but, like many of us, Sudip didn't know how to link philanthropic work with his career and have enough money to live. Sudip was only twenty-two, he was living with his family in a rural village, and had a very different education to that of Bryan or me. Yet, here we were, all with similar values, intentions, and desires for the world around us. This young man had more emotional intelligence and ambition than half the people I knew!

Once we reached back to the house and relaxed for a bit, Bryan and I had a chance to speak about the day. We decided that the situation was horrible, that these people are like extended family to me, and that they deserved a hand. We weren't blind to the fact that we were in a country where a lot of families are affected like this, and I am sure many others were even worse off, but this was our connection, and we felt obliged to offer our service in any way we could. We agreed that we would rebuild the home for them. We would tell them to get their government funding, which they were entitled to, but we would cover the rest. However, as we live in Abu Dhabi, it would be hard to trust anyone here to do the work. The universe though had offered us everything we required in that one trip. We spoke with Sudip and asked how he would feel about working for us for six months, at least. He would be paid to be our project manager on the ground. We would send him the money to manage the work, and he would see the family, the site, deal with any contractors and government bodies, and be our eyes and ears on the ground. To say that he was excited was an understatement. You could see the purpose that suddenly gleamed from his eyes. We were not only going to offer this family a new home; we had begun a journey with this young man who was feeling lost and purposeless.

I am happy to say, one year on, we successfully finished the house and had maintained a great friendship with Sudip, who is also working on other projects with us close to his village. This story, while it makes me so happy to know we could do something for these people, is for me an example of what I mean when I say we are all responsible for one another in our global community. We could have seen that they were without a house and heard the faint hope of a government grant and been "ok" with it. We could have listened to Sudip and his stories and thought that we have all been there and he will find a way. But instead, we decided that, given we have access to resources for a project like this, it is up to us to help bring it to life. It was our responsibility to help these people in whatever way we could. It didn't take much from us, outside of cash and guidance, both of which we had plenty to offer. And the effects, well, they speak for themselves.

Looking at this story, we are no different to anyone else. The funding for the house and Sudip's salary came from the salary I earned while I was still in the corporate world. I had no fallback plan, no organization, no religious purpose with it. I had an obligation and the main lesson for me during this time was to **serve as best as I could within the capacity that was available to me**. The community may be thousands of miles from where I live, but the connection, the impact, and lasting effects I felt knowing that I could be part of a solution is almost unexplainable. It didn't take a huge resource, a large team, or even a great deal of planning. I saw an opportunity to serve and I took it. It simply took courage to accept my responsibility in this moment and for that I am eternally grateful.

We are a global community. Each of our problems, while large and diverse, are all of our responsibility. It doesn't mean we feel burdened by them or overwhelmed. It also doesn't imply we go out seeking to solve every problem we see. But when the universe places a situation in front of you like the one we encountered in Nepal, it is for a reason. Each of us need to look outside of ourselves and offer just a piece of us to each other. Whether it is as simple as proposing to help write a resume for someone who may be previously unemployed due to social issues, all the way to funding an entire community development program. No matter what it is, if we all did these constant acts of service, imagine what the world would look like.

WE FIND YOUR PURPOSE.
WE CREATE YOUR BUSINESS.

All of my lessons have been significant, and with hindsight, I am sure they feel more profound than they did at the time. But little did I know, the universe was setting me up for my most significant discovery yet as I reached my thirty-year milestone. In between all of this chaos with work, trying to find my way through what every day threw at me, the universe was placing stepping-stones that I was not yet aware of. These steps, while insignificant at the time, were paramount to guide me on my current path.

During 2016, my "itch" for change was ramping up again, and I was struggling to fit in the corporate mold any longer. I had found that I was losing my usual spirit and excitement for what I do, and much of my time away from work was spent self-indulging to make up for the amount of anger and lack of inspiration and joy I was feeling in my day-to-day work. It doesn't mean I went to work outwardly miserable every day, but the internal dialogue was wearing me down.

At this stage, I was living in Abu Dhabi, and like many expat cities, it was a great place to work as a young, single person. It was vibrant, full of people from different backgrounds, and an excellent stomping ground to grow my network. During my first six months of moving there in 2013, I met two guys from Australia, Stephen and Keith, who had created their own food and beverage brand in Abu Dhabi. It was the first of its kind, creating an all-day dining concept with some of our Australian favorites. I originally met the boys at their restaurant, which was near to my house, and we hit it off from day one. Stephen and I got along exceptionally well, as I was drawn to his eccentric and creative personality, and loved how he looked at the world as if anything was possible. Stephen went to university, but enjoyed the social life of it more than the work (as he will tell you), then spent the rest of his working life as an entrepreneur. Literally, he had not spent a day in the corporate world. We used to laugh as he would ask me, "What are you even typing about all day long?" I thought it was the funniest thing in the world, as it is so accurate. What was I typing about all day long? On average in my last role, I would receive three-hundred-plus emails a day and send over a hundred myself.

Over the years, and by 2016, the boys and I would hang out and have conversations about their current brands and new ones they were looking to open. It was exciting and, not knowing it at the time, my future self resonated with these discussions given the changes that would come for me. As our relationships grew, we got to know one another well, and we would spend a considerable amount of time together. Stephen would tell me how he loved my ideas and our creativity bounced off one another, especially after a few wines. We enjoyed it so much that I started working with them on weekends to develop different concepts, so we could pitch to investors. He would call me with a new idea, and in one phone call, it would turn into this incredible concept that we would both be buzzing about after. I even put together a mood board early on (a collage of photos and ideas to bring the concept to life), not knowing that's what I was doing, and the boys loved it. They found a natural flair in me, and were working to help bring that out. I was being introduced into Stephen's world and it excited me. I loved the creative branch I was being offered, which suddenly made my world of logistics, management, and corporate life look very stale.

Little did I know, this work of creating concepts would actually lead to the formation of our current company, and my new source of service, Blonde and Bear. The process I undertook began to shape me for a life I hadn't even envisioned yet. It was preparing me for the changes ahead. All I could do at the time was see it as something minor that I was excited about, but I never thought it would eventuate, as I was not "qualified" for the work.

Stephen and Keith both inspired me in their own ways, showing me a part of my world I didn't know yet. The relationship between Stephen and I was unique and the beginning to a flame that was going to burn bright. He showed me what I wanted in the world. He encouraged me to light that flame and watch it burn, to not be afraid of being myself, and to use creativity to my advantage. He introduced me to people that were successful in what they do and who inspired me, including his own Aunty and Uncle who are amazing and highly influential business people in Australia. I will cherish the five hours I had the privilege to spend with them in Sydney until my last days.

It is not often that I meet people who would inspire me so profoundly, in a way that I think I have not yet had with anyone else. The way they viewed the world with such possibility; the entrepreneurial mind-set they lived in that drove their desire to build companies from scratch and create developments in the country that would benefit the people and the economy; an attitude that led to some of the most wonderful stories and exciting adventures. Maybe it was my future self resonating at that moment, or a deep gut instinct that was telling me, "This information is good, Luke"—but either way, it mattered, and I felt it.

In November 2016, Bryan and I were in Bali, Indonesia, for the UAE National Day holidays. I had holiday leave to use up for the year, and I wasn't sure how much longer I had at EY, so I thought we best make the most of it. We had booked in for two nights at the Four Seasons Ubud, a spectacular property in the heart of the Balinese rainforest, before heading down to Seminyak. Our villa overlooked the raging river that ran through the grounds—it was stunning. During the day we enjoyed the benefits of the villa and laid by the pool, chatting, writing, and winding down. Between our last trip to Nepal last month and this trip to Bali, I had a potential business idea that I had been working on with friends which was getting close to fruition but it fell short of my expectations. The idea itself was exciting and saw us creating a new hotel brand that took the industry to a new level, but the setup, structure, and people involved made me feel like I wouldn't be stepping out of corporate and into an exciting entrepreneurial role. Instead, I would be sidestepping and working for another start-up company, filled with its own politics and with no major influence of my own. I had always envisioned working for myself as being light and fun. I had an image of waking each day and being filled with drive to grow the business further, and see the impact I could have on the community. Rather, this new prospect for the hotel brand, while it felt like that in the beginning, began to feel difficult, complicated, and simply not right. Most people would just suck it up and proceed or veto the idea. But this was my real chance to make a change in my career and work toward this dream of having my own business for the first time. So, I was feeling down about what the future looked like.

I was chatting with Bryan in Ubud, Bali, and he offered me another idea. "What if we were to open a consulting company that worked with entrepreneurs to help them to create their business? I mean, I do it already as part of my interior design company, and you are great at concepts, understand branding, experience, and business culture—we could have a business that worked just for that purpose," he said. "Business concept design—supporting entrepreneurs to bring their dreams to life. It's missing in the market."

I was rattled. What? This couldn't work? Why would people pay us for that type of work? And what do I even know about concept design? I had created a few concepts over the last year or so, and I had worked for some major brands myself, but surely that didn't qualify me to start charging for it?

We discussed the idea in detail, and I started to see what he was saying. As I began to get on board, offering my own thoughts on how we could do this, the idea changed and transformed. What if we were to create a business that took what we are both good at? Something where we could help people find their purpose through a service where the outcome is a business concept created to both make money and bring that person further joy. Once this clicked, the ideas started to flood in.

At the end of our four-day trip to Bali, our new business concept design service, Blonde and Bear, had been formed. The name came to us after writing a fairy tale for the concept of a boy who is lost in the darkness and finds his light with the help of a magical and gentle bear. (You can find the story at the end of this chapter.) By the end of December, our ideas were being cemented in, and I started to tell the family about what we had planned to do. In January, we met our local business partner in the UAE, who not only loved the idea but also wanted to come on board. Being a dynamic and well-known entrepreneur herself, it was without question that we would work with her. Blonde and Bear would remain Bryan and I, but she would be our UAE ambassador.

Before we knew it, January had arrived, and I was so devoted to Blonde and Bear that I could no longer focus on my corporate job. The "itch" was too intense, and my gut was telling me that this will work and to just take the risk, despite many of my friends saying how much they were hesitant of the idea. I decided that I am employable, I was over my job, and worst case, I could go back to Australia or move companies if it falls over. I am twenty-eight, I told myself, what is the worst that could happen? I resigned. I was freaking out inside when I did. And my boss, also a good friend, just came out with a few expletives that I won't share here, but I knew he was sad to see me go. And so began the winding down of my corporate life as I leapt into the unknown.

On February 7th, 2017, we launched the website and the company. We were in action, and we already had five clients through our local partner. Five clients! Surely this was a good sign. By March I was finished with the airline and jumped into the entrepreneurial life. In the beginning, I saw Blonde and Bear as my chance to step away from what I knew and take on a different way of working. It was a chance to offer myself over full-time in a creative world that I craved while working one-on-one with clients, which I knew I was good at. Little did I know that this would be the beginning of understanding service in all that we do.

For the first month of work, it felt more like I was on a holiday. I had work to do, which we did, and the creative process took it out of me. My God, we would do one creative session to conceptualize some ideas, and I would be knocked out for the rest of the afternoon. The reality of working creatively is underrated. It is tiring, and you need to be connected to your highest self in order to be able to muster up the best ideas. It felt like I was an old flute that was out of tune and required service. My mind was like an overweight person stepping into the gym for the first time, so it was no wonder that I struggled for a couple of months at the start. The ideas would come, and we impressed our clients, but it came at a cost. I was used to the demands of the corporate world, which is job first and you second, so I was pushing myself and beating myself up when I did get exhausted. Thankfully, I had Bryan with me who had been doing this for years. He was kind, as always, and explained that it would be exhausting. We would literally come up with an entire concept for a business in two hours and then finish the work in a day. This would include three different names and logo concepts, five key business differentials for the brand, plus target market and brand purpose, as well as concepts for the look and feel (either collateral or interiors, depending on the brand). The aim of our work was to create a branding guideline that a company could use as their own guide and a guide for others assisting them in creating their business. Too often people start businesses without thinking through their purpose from the start. And before they know it, they have a business that may not reflect what they truly wanted. This approach allowed them to have a guideline, and access to two people who cared functioning as their unofficial business partners.

How we created these concepts in such short time is an entirely different section of the book, or maybe another book altogether (actually, Elizabeth Gilbert's *Big Magic* sums it up beautifully). But we managed to do it. Like all jobs, I slowly settled into this new way of working. The habit of waking up and rushing to my computer first thing to answer emails and check in for work was actually really hard to drop. After the holiday period finished, it became difficult to understand what I had to do and when. No one pulls you up on things or asks you to complete work. Your success, and ultimately, your failure, is all a result of what you put in. I recall reading this previously in some quote, and the thought pushes you to an extent. But when I was working for someone else, if I didn't want to work or had an *off* day, it just meant I didn't get something done. A quick apology, finish it the next day, and it was fine. Now, if I didn't do something, it could mean losing a client altogether and no apology will win that back.

Bryan explained one thing to me that made a lot of sense: the first three to six months of running your own business is like being a high school student experiencing university for the first time. You suddenly realize that you won't get in trouble for not going to class, you can choose to do what you want with your day and, sometimes, to do nothing will be way more appealing (and likely the option you take). He said, don't be harsh on yourself about it. Just be mindful that this is how your mind is working. Each day, just focus on getting small amounts of work done. A few hours of focus is better than eight hours of lazy, halfhearted work. This really resonated with me. And I found that a few hours of committed work may be less than what I deluded myself to believe I did in the office, but way more productive than I would ever do on a daily basis.

Starting your own business is tough going. It has costs that you don't expect and requires you to be switched on for long periods of time. It demands things of you, without you even asking for it. And it relies on your own commitment to stay alive. I had a choice every day. Focus on the work and ensure its survival, or let it fail and go back to what I didn't like before. I knew what my option would be.

Once we had started to find a rhythm in work, we also began to see the types of clients that resonated toward our brand and the kind of support that they required. Surprisingly, in the UAE, we were working with mostly Emirati women. These women are powerful. After so many years of being quiet and submissive to traditional culture, they have a fire in their belly and humility in their heart, and they are determined. With passion and a desire to succeed, we have seen some of the shyest women create brands and find real purpose in what they do each day. For me, it also meant finding my own version of service from this new platform. I was now in a position where I could work with people one-to-one, from the heart, and find strategic ways to activate them and bring their ideas to life.

Previously, I believed that we would have to find one job that suits our needs. A job and a company that would take care of my constantly changing and varied ideas and emotions. However, what I found is that no single company or position can do this. Even creating our own brand only gave me an opportunity to offer one part of myself through service. What I have found is that through a more flexible lifestyle, I was able to use my writing as a tool for service too, beginning my own blog site at www.helloiamluke.com. Here, I would offer my experiences as a young entrepreneur and give real-world insight into the feelings and experiences of taking on a challenge like this. Beyond my writing, I found that I could start investing in businesses and offer personal mentoring to people who required support in finding their own passions and seeking a different view of the world. I discovered, and I liked to share, that if you want a different perspective of the world, then just change your own. This shift in perception can have incredible power in your life, as it is what truly defines our reality.

There were a million lessons that came my way during this time—whether it was the daily intricacies of running a business (let alone running it in a foreign country); the difficulties of red tape and bureaucracy for SME businesses in a developing country; or the constant challenge of balancing your dreams with overcoming your own personal doubts and uncertainties. The list is long. But my main lesson from this experience has been learning how to **redefine risk.** So many people I know spoke about how much of a risk I was taking by leaving my perfectly comfortable job and stepping out on my own. And that's fair; it was a big call. But it certainly wasn't a risk. A risk would mean that what I had was more than enough—that I was challenged, happy, and secure—all of which weren't true. I had tackled the challenges that existed for me and didn't crave anything further from that company. I was far from happy in my role, and security is more of a mind-set than a reality. I could have been booted from that job any day of the week for all I know! Yet, so many people truly believe that this idea of risk exists. We use it as a barrier to keep us from chasing our dreams. But it simply isn't true. Yes, if you have a family to support, you need to be mindful of the risks you take to ensure that they are at least calculated. But I was twenty-eight years old. In the worst case, I wouldn't make money in my new venture, would struggle for a minute, and then would get another corporate job and try again. Where is the risk in that? We are all employable and we are all capable of stepping back into what we once did, if our next steps don't work out as we hope. To believe in risk means to be believe in fear. Yes, you should be smart about your moves and understand the right approach financially and emotionally, but if the universe has given you an "itch" to chase, and when you chase it, everything begins to fall in line, isn't that enough? I trust in the abundance of the universe that has delivered me to where I stand today, and know that it is waiting to continue to deliver the same abundance in my future.

ITCH

PART TWO –
REDEFINING HOW TO LIVE

As I turn the page to my third decade of life and reflect back on my experiences so far, I reflect back on my journey and the stories that I have created, which have shaped the person I am today. These experiences have been integral in broadening my understanding of who I am, what I stand for, how I perceive the world, and how I can serve those around me. They have been part of my slow uncovering of my authentic self, and have created the reality that shaped the person I am today—whether that be physically, spiritually, mentally, or emotionally. But, what do these lessons have in common? What has been a common theme for me in my life so far? What have I experienced over and again, that I know so many other people continue to undergo as part of our shared human reality? Well, for me, those recurrent themes would be spirituality and purpose.

These two themes, which are major parts of all of our lives, have shown me and continue to show me more about myself, my soul, and my connection to the world. They have been the lights in my path to my authentic self, and they have shown me that I have only scratched the surface of what I need to understand. They have shaped who I am, because I have learned that at my core, this is all we are—purpose-led spiritual beings having a human experience and driven by the power of love. But what do these two things look like? Do we all perceive them in the same way? Or is this a truly personal discovery that each of us must find out for ourselves? Could there be a formula that we can use to uncover these or are they hidden gems that we must use this life to uncover for our own growth?

Until now, my story has been everyday events that have shaped me. I have allowed life to happen, and for me to be the observer—experiencing the story and looking back, reflecting on the lessons along the way. I find that many people in life do this, well, for most of their lives. Sit back and allow life to take control. I know I did it for a lot of my own. But through sitting back and allowing life to take the reins, I have learned that I hand myself over to believing that what I experience is simply "life" and that I must go along with it. What I have come to realize though, in my most recent personal journey, is that I don't have to accept life as it is. In fact, I have every right, as does every soul in this human experience, to reshape, remold, and redefine my own perspectives and experiences on what these common themes could mean and how I interact with them.

What if I said that the reason so many of us couldn't find the answers to some of our biggest questions is because we aren't willing to look for these answers outside of our existing framework? What if I said that the reason some of us feel unfulfilled when it comes to spirituality or purpose is because they are linked and require one in order to have the other? For so many years, I had a belief that I had to merely receive the information from spiritual teachers, religious leaders, and gurus alike, in order to find out more about the spiritual aspects of the human experience. But, in actual fact, I have learned that I am the master of my own teachings, and have every power to empty my own spiritual cup of old dogmas and doctrines, old fractured ways of thinking, and ask questions to define a higher power for myself. And through this process, I have actually found a way to redefine not only my core beliefs, but also the very drive I need on a daily basis—my purpose.

I want to take you now on a slightly different journey, still through my own self-discovery, but a journey that has taken me from a two-dimensional view of purpose and spirituality, flawed in old beliefs and understandings, to a slightly more expansive and personal definition of what these stand for in the current space of where I am today. I want to begin to redefine two of my greatest themes in life—to seek a clearer and more profound understanding for myself, challenge cultural norms that I and other friends I have spoken to have battled with along the way, and find power in asking questions that for so long, I either didn't think I could ask or felt that I was not capable of asking. I want to show people that through redefining your core beliefs, you will see a powerful effect on your daily purpose. I want to begin to redefine these themes, and I say "begin," as life is truly an ever-evolving journey, in order to continue to shape a life that truly matters, uncover my deepest "itch," and ultimately continue on the path to discover my most authentic self.

REDEFINING SPIRTUALITY

The very conversation about the theme of spirituality has brought about a range of different emotions and responses from me over the years. Everything from understanding it as something I engage with when and if I feel like it, to the reality of believing in ghosts, receiving clairvoyant readings, energy healings, past-life conversations, the idea of karma, a rejection of a traditional religious path to God, learning to trust in my own gut intuition, and so on. These types of conversations were the realities of this spiritual self that I thought I understood. It was something light, unknown, and somewhat mystical. It played on that part of my brain that enjoyed watching movies and fantasizing about a future that is well beyond where I stood in that moment. It never hurt anyone, I kept getting on with my day job, and it allowed for some interesting reading at times. But the concepts as they stood were always flawed, left my rational mind feeling confused, and didn't really "add" anything to my life. It was something that I thought some of us may have a lot of in life, while many others won't. But either way, it was another segmented part of this reality.

In fact, spirituality has been one of my greatest "itches" throughout my life, especially within the last twelve years. It has been a place of unknowns and frustrations at times. The idea that something far greater than us exists, but cannot be proven, always bothered me—but I never felt equipped to try to understand it more fully, as the texts and practices that surrounded it never appeased my rational mind. I resisted the idea that we have to connect to a version of ourselves that is calm and internal, which for a young man filled with ego sounds like a complete bore. Or the idea that we have to engage in a world where, for the most part, we can only see destruction and confrontation, or a room full of people who are trying so hard to be this enlightened version of themselves, only to find they, too, are riddled with emotional turmoil and baggage. When I looked at the notion of spirituality from the world of my ego, I could never understand why I would want to or need to engage in what it had to offer. However, through years of that "itch" not disappearing, I began my own journey of reconnection—not of discovery, as that would dictate that we don't possess some connection to our spiritual self in the first place. Instead, I believe that our spiritual self, this "self" that many spend their lives in search of, is there from the moment we are born, and part of our journey is simply to reconnect to this space. This reconnection was one where I took it on in the same way I take on everything else in my life—questioning why it exists in the framework that it does. In reconnecting to this space, I battled with so many old frameworks that I had created in my mind. And through breaking down these old patterns of thought and jaded perspectives, what I seemed to find is a few new theories, some new perspectives, and a journey on the path to my own version of this thing called "God."

The Old Ways Are Broken

One of the most difficult parts of my spiritual quest has been accepting that the old way in which we work is broken. I have seen this in my career and my relationships even more expansively across our global society... the way in which we have operated for so many years is fractured and we are struggling to make ends meet on a number of levels. The way we connect with one another, the work we do on a daily basis, the economic system we operate within, our spiritual connection to our highest source—it is all fractured. For many, whilst they may still be perceived as "working," they are not creating an environment of growth for mankind. Even the basic fact that man and woman are still not equal in the true sense of equality (and not a set of statistics or sociopolitical debate) is a fracture within our society and within our spiritual makeup. But why do we accept this? Why are we so scared to question and challenge the ways as they stand now? Why is it that we are so scared to challenge man when he stands before us with spiritual text and attempts to play a mere mortal version of God within society? Why is it we are accepting that one person's interpretation on the text of our prophets is the only way to interpret it? Why is it that once we reject the old ways of religion, we think we are only left with spirituality in the form of yoga and meditation, crystals, and incense, and not in any other forms? Why is it that we have been so defected by the impacts of human ritualistic behavior when it comes to religion that we have gone to the other extreme and said that only science is the answer? Why is it that we are all not doing our own search for our own version of God? A God that offers specific messages through all of our prophets for us to personally sit with and understand? A God that works in a world that is in fact built on traditional science and quantum physics? A God that works through you in the form of prayer and service? A God that speaks to you through fitness, yoga, and music as much as through prayer and meditation? Why is it we simply disregard this major element of our life, to focus on our self, our material possessions, and our worldly ways, only to find that we are more lost, more disconnected, and more depressed than ever before? This is not about telling people their ways are wrong either. If they have found their version of this and it works, fantastic. If it truly works within the love and guidance of what their God speaks about, then that is their own prerogative. The other option is to find what you believe to be true—your version of God, or the universe, or the quantum field of reality, or whatever you need to call it, the same as I have begun to do myself. This is one of my biggest lessons, the driving force behind writing this book, and part of how I have begun to understand and master so many fundamental areas in my life.

Unblocking My Spiritual Growth

Over time, the one thing that I have learned is that my most profound spiritual growth had occurred only when I was capable of either understanding the meaning of a particular spiritual concept/word/idea, or when I chose to redefine what that concept meant for me. As I mentioned before, my own relationship with God has changed over the years, and previously just that term alone would make me shudder. The idea that to be with "God" meant that I was seeking a structured, ritualistic faith that believed, ultimately, that a man was ruling my world and science didn't really have the answers. To me, that was *absolute* bollocks. So, I went to the other end of the spectrum, disregarding faith, destroying the notion of religion, and certainly never referring to all that existed beyond our capacity as this three-letter word of *God*.

At the same time, I would seek spirituality for my belief system. However, this too was flawed. Not in what I learned, but in the fractures in which this information was offered. I believed the universe held a more significant meaning than what we understood it to, but not that hideous preexisting idea of "God" and everything that came with it. I thought it meant that we were built from the cosmos and that we existed from one point in time, as that we just exploded from nothing. I believed that "everything happened for a reason," and that we were guided by the universe, whatever that was. But at times, we, as conscious beings, would go off course and the universe would almost punish us for doing this (old fragments of hearing the traditional religious stories created for law and order in times before our current civilization). I thought prayer related back to this same old notion of God, but I would meditate because that was a better thing to do than "pray." I also thought prayer was hopeless, because, again, I would look at those who had blind faith in religion, and would surrender with no control to something that was also fractured. Basically, my whole perception of what I believed was riddled with a lack of depth and understanding. In fact, I also went beyond both of these and just opted to be an atheist at one point, as I figured that science at least gave my rational mind an opportunity to tangibly understand our existence and leave all the other mumbo jumbo for those who are happy to walk blindly into life. However, like before, when I started stepping into the world with this new rigid view, I found that no matter how deep the conversation, I would come across so many examples that were classified "unknown." Things that, potentially for all we know, may never have a way for humans to explain in our limited world of experience and language.

Lastly, my final point toward my original rejection of religion and God related back to my sexuality. Even to this day, many people who deem themselves religious genuinely believe that my sexuality is a choice and a sin. They preach that we are all children of their God, however, should we not meet their criteria of what that person should look like, then they threw you to the side and call you a defect. They demonize you and reject you from the community. They speak with such hatred in the name of God and make us believe that this is the view of the creator. And yet, despite knowing in our hearts that this is wrong, we listen to them. We look to scared men and women standing on their perch, preaching to their own community through their own interpretation of an ambiguous spiritual text, to ensure that their own limited views of the world are not challenged. It is heartbreaking. And it is no wonder that so many people around the world are rejecting the notion of religion altogether, not to mention minority groups like the gay community, who have been fundamentally told that they do not belong. Just to add some perspective, it would be like saying you chose to be a white man. It just makes no sense. But I am not here to talk poorly of other people's views. These are just the reasons why I rejected these ideas on my own path, and yet, have come back to my own version of God.

So, what have I done to find this? What could possibly be the next steps for someone who has rejected religion, created a strange relationship with a thing called spirituality, but also believes that science matters? Did I suddenly find the answer in yet another cult-like religion? Or maybe I met God himself and got the answer? Of course, none of this happened. But what I did is I decided to start again. I decided to take a different approach from before, and through meeting different people in my life (my incredible partner, Bryan, for one), I decided to reset what I knew and start from scratch.

What did I know for sure up until this moment?
I knew that I had a bad relationship with the word "God."
I knew that I didn't fundamentally agree with the concept of organized religion as it existed throughout history.
I knew that the term "universe" offered me what I think I would get from the word "God," but it was still too vague.
I knew that spirituality offered me some connection with my highest self, but again, was filled with so many people and ideas that it had no real factual basis that would appease my rational mind.
I knew that I loved what science could offer, and felt that there was room for it in the equation too, but not on its own.
I knew that we all had something that connected us that was beyond our physical selves, and through years of developing this composite thing called language, we just had to figure out what was the same amongst so many and where we were letting ourselves down.
I knew that there was more to life, and that any behaviors that were selfish or self-serving never brought about true joy.
I knew that a real, deep-rooted sense of joy mattered.

So what next? Where do I go from here? Well, while this sounds like it was some realization I had overnight, much like coming out, it was not. This was a culmination of what I was feeling but wasn't entirely conscious of in the haze of confusion that hung over my head. However, as it was part of what I had to learn, I was offered all the right teachers and experiences to get me to where I am now, and I know this will continue for the many years to come.

The first step to understanding this better was to redefine how I engaged with the words that caused friction for me. Like all things in life, if you are battering against the winds, then something is not right for you. So why did I have such a bad relationship with these words? What was it about "God" and "religion" that rubbed me up the wrong way? Was it the fact that I saw the anger and divide it was bringing to the world over so many years? Was it that it represented a blind belief that no longer made sense in our modern society? Was it that, fundamentally, all of the major religions believed that as a gay man, despite my values and all the service I offered to people in our global community, my sexuality and choice of person to love is a "sin"? And, ultimately, in the realms of their belief of heaven and hell, that I would be going straight to the afterlife of despair as I was made defected. Or was it that this same thing that drove all of us, this term "God," was telling me that what we see now and how we are treated isn't right, that it is the result of man and his ego, and to follow my intuition to find what will serve me over time?

I took these words, and I broke them. I challenged myself to start looking into them. To look at religion from every aspect, including internally. To begin to study different parts of theology and the word of prophets who have come down over our time. To remove the need for labels and to assign ourselves to a particular belief, much like how I hate being defined by my sexuality, and see the world more logically. I mean, we have had some different prophets come to this earth with ultimately the same message and refreshed views each time. They came down to us during particular periods of despair in mankind, and they offered a message from a source that is beyond our human existence. With that message came new inspiration for growth in humanity. It brought the people of that time new laws and perceptions. It brought an understanding of our own morbid existence so that we could evolve beyond where we stood, and into the state we are today. These prophets delivered messages of hope and love; they brought insight into who they were, how they were connected to those that stood before them and those that will follow. They brought with them an opportunity for us to listen. And at the same time, our human evolution has progressed to allow our minds to accept this new idea of a separate God or entity. Science shows us that we evolved to comprehend an unknown entity, and history shows that we have prophets who came to assist in the moral, ethical, and spiritual evolution of man. However, as humans driven by ego and emotion, all parts of the physiological makeup that makes each of us, we oversaw this, bought into only what we understood with our limited minds and education, and created belief systems that are used not only to guide us, but also to control us.

At the same time I broke down these words, I thought about what I experienced every day, and the different books and theories I have read that show these same messages, branches of these messages, or inspiration occurring in our everyday life. I looked at the concept of prayer and why I thought this was a waste of time. I mean, for many who have a religious belief, they would almost laugh and feel sorry for "someone like me" who didn't believe in something as powerful as prayer. But what did this even mean? Was it that the idea of prayer insinuated that I was therefore religious, and well, we all know how I feel about that? Or was it that I was scared of the power it may have when I felt that I didn't have the clearest direction? Or was it that prayer indicated speaking outwardly to something that was external to me, and even that idea didn't feel right?

On the flip side to this, I spoke about how "spiritual" I was and how connected I felt to the universe. But what did this mean? And why had I built up a belief in my life to feel so safe and comfortable with understanding this notion of spirituality? Was it that I had experienced what people would call supernatural moments in my life that only the realm of "spirituality" could accept or define? Was it that I had experienced the power of kinesiology in resolving health issues as a child, and saw the benefits of a holistic approach to life which I felt I couldn't get otherwise? Was it that the term "spirituality," which was the alternative "go-to" for many who had rejected the old ways of religion, was just more open to all things that we couldn't once define? Yet, despite having this open space and freedom to believe what felt "right" as opposed to what I was told to be right, the moment I would talk about what the "universe" stands for, my theories would be flawed. It is all well and good to say that we just need to meditate and see what comes to us, but if we meditate for hours and then go and read some empty quote on social media, that doesn't make for a more enlightened person. The spiritual guru down the road may have had some of his or her own insight, but that doesn't mean that he or she is all-seeing and all-knowing. That same guru, while maybe allowing for some more reading of text and meditation, is still as human as you and me. What makes them more knowledgeable than, say, a prophet? Oh, I remember: the word of a prophet means I need to buy into that thing called religion—and so the cycle begins.

Once I broke these down for myself to understand, over a series of experiences and teachings from different people in my life I decided to redefine what these words meant to me personally. And so I did. After researching and evolving my own knowledge, to a point where I emptied my own cup and began refilling it with things that genuinely fit for now, I came up with the below definitions. These definitions are open to any person's interpretation, but this is what I understand, at this moment, to be right for me:

GOD - All that is—life's essence. That which can be seen in the attributes of all things, but never understood or comprehended in its purest state.
DIVINE SOURCE - Another term for God. The energy which we call love.
PRAYER - Our conversation with our highest source or God, and our own connection to that source.
SPIRITUALITY - The relationship we hold with that which is beyond our human existence – beyond what we comprehend as material. It is what we are born with before any man made 'religious' acts or identities are created. True spirituality for me is your generosity, your kindness, your energy you bring to a space. It is your innate human virtues, like love, compassion and empathy. And it can also be expressed within the material world through cleanliness and beauty.
RELIGION - Traditionally, a human construct for the purpose of faith and guidance based on the word of the most recent prophet; a way in which community was previously built and the word of God was offered to that community in order to help humankind progress. For me, it's an opportunity to create unity among humankind. For without unity, religion holds no purpose.
UNIVERSE - The alternative word used for "God," to allow those that do believe in something non-material, something beyond themselves, but are tired of the broken perceptions of all that is beyond what we can comprehend.
MEDITATION - The way to listen to God and the universe, the way our prayers are answered, and a connection to that of our highest source. The human capacity for stillness, to clear the mind and connect with our divine source—detaching from human experience, to seek refuge and guidance from our soul.
SOUL - The spirit of man and the light of our most authentic self. That which already exists and evolves in dimensions beyond what we can comprehend and that which is seeking to evolve within this realm of the human existence.
SPIRIT - The same as our rational soul. The energy of our spiritual self. Many prophets refer to the holy spirit, as that of the force of God. This is our own individual energy of God.
HEAVEN - A religious term; in the example of the afterlife, it was what some people believed would be the place where our life, based on religious law, would be judged and rewarded. For me, it is a metaphor used to describe the type of life we experience now through joy and service.
HELL - The same as heaven in terms of others interpretations of the afterlife, but for me it is what we now know as a life of ego and selfish behavior;

lacking in service, and filled with pain and suffering that is not used to evolve ourselves. It is a world lacking joy, and most evidently, lacking grace.

PROPHET - Human beings who were chosen for a divine purpose, and who channeled what they call the "Holy Spirit." Those who were offered a message from our divine source, known as God, beyond anything our human minds can comprehend, with the most substantial capacity for guidance and love to shift and shape mankind for centuries. They can be understood as our divine physicians, or our Divine Teachers, sent one after another, to guide us through this human experience.

Now, before we continue on, for many people, you may be bombarded with a plethora of different thoughts reading this. Those that hold religious beliefs may feel under attack, as my views may challenge your own. Those that hold no beliefs, including even spiritual beliefs, will likely be rolling their eyes and questioning why we have gone to that word "God." And some may be finding solace and insight through my own views for themselves. The one thing that this shows, and that which I have learned, is that regardless of whether you agree or disagree, it doesn't matter. Why? Because it is about my own journey. It is the journey of my own reality to understand the deeper meanings to life, and to create something that ultimately offers me what I perceive to be as growth and understanding. And on a basic human level, it is to bring me joy. A type of joy where I can release myself of those things which we say exist in this term called "hell" and create a life that is built of what we would imagine to be "heaven." That is my freedom and my prerogative in my life. As much as it is your very own.

OK, so what does this all mean? Well over this same time, I have managed to fill a cup that is built on two very important fundamentals in life: spirituality and science. A cup that continues to offer many answers and insights along my journey. It shows me what makes up this reality we live in, and it gives me insight into those things that cannot be explained in this reality or even in this time, because the source of that unknown is far beyond the realms in which we exist, or our current understandings and scientific capacities cannot reach its theories. It gives me an opportunity to understand this world in ways that are far deeper than just being defined by your sexuality. It gives me greater purpose. And once we tap into this depth, superficial things like seeking "likes" for your photo on social media diminish, the need to seek out multiple sexual partners for gratification begins to disappear, the fear of chasing your dreams changes into a desire to want to offer more of yourself to the world. It is a space where your values are strengthened, your childlike intrigue of the world reignites, and you start to see magic all around you.

To understand more and to seek growth, you first need to empty your cup of unsubstantiated ideas and theories that you once held. If the information you once believed is in fact true to its source, you won't lose it. But if it is not, you gracefully allow for it to be removed so that our divine source can replenish it with only that which will help you.

The Study of Theology and Science
As I have said, when it comes to spirituality, I believe that a diverse approach to what our spiritual outlook looks like is important. And, for me, this has come through the recent study of both theology and science, on top of my existing spiritual knowledge. Why? Because when I look at the world around me, I see each of these worlds, when they stand alone, as fractured. As much as theology believes it has the answer, it doesn't hold all the answers to life in this human experience we live in. It does when it comes to the essence of God, all that is beyond us and which we cannot explain. But it doesn't have the answers to, say, *What is reality? What is this human experience, in its truest essence, before soul and spirit become part of the equation to create a conscious explorer of the space? What are emotions and why do they have such a profound impact on us both physically and spiritually? How does the nurturing of the spirit assist with the nurturing of the physical form, to provide a prolonged human experience?* These are the types of questions, in my mind, that really matter. And ignorance, much like the ignorance of other humans toward, say, my sexuality, is what stops our capacity for evolution and growth. It is our responsibility to seek the information we need to develop and transform within our lifetime. And who knows, with this new knowledge, others may come up with a theory of their own that will change the course of history as we know it. Better yet, they may even find that at one point in the near future science and religion—not in the framework as we understand them to be right now, but with more depth and investigation—will be one and the same.

The Language of Our World
It's a funny thing, language. We understand it in the purest form—a way in which we can create dialogue to communicate with each other. But, the one thing I have learned is that language is not just the formation of symbols and sounds to create a way in which to communicate between each other. No, the power of language is beyond shaping a sound, or making a noise to express a gesture, or writing a symbol on a piece of paper. We are far beyond

this. Language has a profound and lasting impact on our spiritual and emotional selves. How you offer those things called "words," matters. The words you choose to communicate with matter. The way in which these words are perceived by others matters too.

We seem to fail to understand the complexity of language and wonder why our fellow man is hurting from a small comment being made, or a remark on the internet. If we think back to when we were children, the idea of bullying hurt us. It was not nice to be told that we were an idiot, or that we were stupid because we didn't know how to do something. However, as we grow up, we seem to forget this impact or become numb to it, and we turn into the grown version of the same bullies who once hurt us. What do I mean by this? Well, I believe we are not conscious enough of the words that we choose to use on a daily basis. Not just the way we speak to a stranger, but more importantly the way we express ourselves to our loved ones. Do you use kind and loving words, even in anger? Do you find ways to tell people how fantastic they are as often or as quickly as you are to say to them that they have annoyed you?

Even amidst conversation with your peers, what type of dialogue do you engage in? Do you speak about the weather, or find a way to fill them in on the self-created drama of your life? Do you speak kindly about people, or do you spend the time passing judgment on those around you? When you write things on social media, are you positive and upbeat, only to find that in real life, you don't engage in kind or meaningful conversation? Or worse, are you the opposite? As we are progressive and intelligent creatures, the way in which we now use the language that we have created over history is even more critical than it was before. In a time of mass communication and connection, we are in such dire need of consciousness in our word more than ever before.

If you were to look at it from a spiritual standpoint, you would find that our prophets have been teaching us this since the earliest records of prophecy. Whether it was one of our earlier prophets, Buddha, which quite simply states...

> *"Better than a thousand hollow words is one word that brings peace."*

Right up to our most recent prophet, Bah'u'allah, who spoke about removing backbiting and gossip from our lives:

"He must never seek to exalt himself above anyone, must wash away from the tablet of his heart every trace of pride and vain-glory, must cling unto patience and resignation, observe silence and refrain from idle talk. For the tongue is a smoldering fire, and excess of speech a deadly poison. Material fire consumeth the body, whereas the fire of the tongue devoureth both heart and soul. The force of the former lasteth but for a time, whilst the effects of the latter endureth a century.

That seeker should, also, regard backbiting as grievous error, and keep himself aloof from its dominion, inasmuch as backbiting quencheth the light of the heart, and extinguisheth the life of the soul."

To think, for so many years, we have been offered these words of advice from many of our most significant spiritual guides, and yet we continue to ignore them. Only to find that as we evolve in technology and connection, our words degrade and our power diminishes.

Sadly, I find in this day and age, people of all backgrounds can all be so consumed with their own lives and that of others, that gossip and backbiting come so effortlessly. A dialogue that does nothing for those involved or those being spoken about. And we have all done it, which is how I can look back at this lesson and share my thoughts. However, it is up to us to choose to be conscious of our words. It is up to us to decide to look at the world, take all of our own insecurities, past hurts, and current emotions, and decide that we will only speak the words that we would want to hear.

Think for a moment about the times you have spent a conversation backbiting and gossiping, versus a time where you have spent it having a meaningful discussion of new ideas and hopeful chatter. Which one left you feeling uplifted and positive, and which one left you feeling worse than when you began the conversation? As science continues to grow and evolve, our own understanding of these spiritual essences will also grow and evolve. What if one day we found out that gossiping really did affect our soul and its progress? Would you still continue wasting time speaking about others or would you think twice before sharing your views?

Love: Our Most Divine Source
We are the sum of all of our existence, and our biggest flaw in this world of potential divides is that we believe we are made up of separate things that are not connected. This even comes down to the fundamentals of our society.

We believe that we are all separate beings, that what we want, what we experience, and where we want to go are all separate to one another. Ultimately though, what I have found through meeting different people from all walks of life is that we are bound by one thing: Love. We just want to love and to be loved. The many various ways we define love, and who we choose to love is part of what brings such great diversity to our existence, but the fact of the matter is that love is what drives all of us. Whether it is through being loved, desiring love, experiencing love in the wrong form, or seeking love… love is the very essence of our existence. It is what I call the essence of "God" or the "universe," and it is what makes us who we are. It is also the defining point of our human experience. No matter who a person is, you will find that love is part of their existence. Whether it is the love of your partner, your children, or love for your life, your beliefs, your well-being… we are all seeking or giving some form of love. It's the one thing that we can't seem to explain, yet we are all craving and desiring it in one form or another. The problem with love in the human experience is that love is ultimately intangible and unconditional. And our human experience is, for the most part, tangible and filled with human-created conditions. We set rules and guidelines around how we expect to experience these things, and this in fact disconnects us from that source. But what if I was to say that the very word, "love," is holding us back from really understanding its power? What if I was to say that through these human conditions of how we believe the word to be expressed, that we are limiting the very capacity that it holds in this universe?

Recently, I was listening to an incredible talk by Steven Phelps—physicist, philosopher, translator, and Bahai speaker. Steven was talking about this idea of love, looking at it from both a scientific and philosophical point of view, and incorporating writings of Baha'u'allah, who is the prophet of the Bahai faith. Using Steven's extensive knowledge and background across multiple spectrums of information, he positioned the concept of love at the intersection of science, philosophy, and religion. He said that he is finding in his research that, "The force of love isn't just the love of thy neighbor. It is the force that connects everything from the atom through to human civilizations. It is the binary force that science speaks about, as well as the binary force that we experience in the human state and it is what connects hearts."

Just read that quote a few times and try and see if you can gain some perspective on the words. "It is the binary force…" The talk also included a discussion around the theory of the limitations of words, stating that the very words we use limit the capacity of truly understanding the depth of a thing, space, idea, or essence. When we place the word "love" on this "thing" we think we all know, we restrict its capacity to the very word itself. But what if the power of love, this "binary force" is in fact scientific? What if it is the very force that connects atoms, which are the baseline for our entire reality? It would then mean that "love" is the connecting force for everything in this universe, and that this idea of love being seen only in our conditional human reality of emotion is almost primitive. It would also make sense why, for millennia, prophets and spiritual gurus have spoken with such reverence about love. It isn't just about peace and harmony as an ideal state; it is about living in a world with equilibrium between light and dark, good and bad, love and hate. If love is the binary force of atoms, and atoms create our entire existence, what does it mean to reject this idea of love? And why is it that deep down, egos and crazy ideologies aside, love is always the answer? It's worth sitting and pondering this idea more deeply and seeking some answers for ourselves from some of the most forward-thinking people of our time like Dr. Phelps.

Whether love is just "love," or it is in fact the binary force of our entire existence, what I have learned in the space of spirituality is that love connects everything. And our limited view on love is the only limitation we face in experiencing the full capacity and beauty of our most divine source.

Suffering Leads to Spiritual Growth
There is this theory in spirituality in which people speak about having to suffer to grow. I have read it in the text of prophets and from different spiritual gurus alike, and in some way, I always felt this idea of suffering must stem from a time in our history where lives were undoubtedly much harder. Or even that for some of us in developed countries, it is no longer part of the journey. But what I have learned over this period of my life is that suffering doesn't have to come in the form of physical ailment, loss of income, house, or possessions. None of that has to occur. However, when I reflect back, I realize that in my most significant moments of growth, I have had to deal with a lot of internal suffering. The suffering of loss in friends, perceptions, previous comforts, routines, work that I once thought brought about joy. These losses may sound petty, but if we remind ourselves that we are only in control of our actions and reactions, and that our perception is all we have to create this reality, then the loss of perception is far more significant and more profound than the loss of, say, a material possession.

When our greatest prophets say that we have to suffer in the name of God, they do not mean that we have to be victims of abuse or physical torment to experience growth in the name of a judgmental and power-hungry God. For some, physical suffering may be part of their reality, and the path that they must work their way through. But for many others, it will be the suffering endured through the internal shift of consciousness that brings us closer on our path to God. In our society right now, this shift is what is causing the most pain and suffering. We have a world that is becoming more connected than ever before, with ideas and realities being shared between people that had previously never been exposed to each other. Existing ideologies are beginning to crack, belief systems are being challenged, adversities and hardships are being shown to the world, and there is an increase in people turning to different forms of alcohol and drugs to cope. Many of us do not know which way to turn. People use this pain to lash out and hurt those around them, while many others fall within, trapped in a world of depression and despair.

Suffering may exist, but it is part of the spiritual growth. To ask for growth without suffering is like asking to live without breathing. Yet, like breathing, we may need it to survive, but we can also control it. Lean into the suffering, and use it to move beyond the pain and into the space of growth. Despite how painful it may be at times, it will only persist if we believe it. I believe that the truth of the suffering, the belief that it is real and that it is here to stay, are what hurts the most. But what if, instead, we understood that it is part of our growth and that it isn't final. Like all things in life, it too will pass. If we wholeheartedly took this concept of suffering, the experience of pain and turmoil caused by the breakdown of our perceived expectations and realities, and chose to see it as a sign from the universe that the path we are on, the thing we have, and the people we share our lives with are as temporary as our own life itself, would the pain persist, or like the waves of an ocean, would they come and go, washing over us at different times? Would we come out each time on the other side, refreshed and relieved to be on the surface? Many things are just a matter of perspective. It is our job to use our own story and experiences and find a version of truth that not only sits well with each of us, but that promotes growth and expansion.

Trust & Gratitude - Two Virtues of Substance
This is quite simple for me. In life, the most important virtue you need is to trust that the universe, God, that which is all of what we know exists, has

your back. This same external force, whatever you wish to label it, that got you to where you are today; the one that created spectacular moments in your past, who offered you some of the best memories you have, is the same one who stands with you right now. It is the same energy that surrounds you and all that you want in this lifetime. So why at this moment would that same force give up on you? Is this the result of listening to the old broken version of what "God" is and how He punishes you? Is it just that you say you know who your God is, but really you are physiologically "addicted" to the current emotional state you find yourself in that it is easier to keep perpetuating it than to break the cycle? Is it that you understand the idea of spiritual suffering, but confuse it with self-affliction to give way to human attention? Some of these statements may sound harsh, but whatever it is that you believe, now is the time to accept that when you look back and put those dots of your life path together, you can trust that the same care, the same love, and the same precision is offered in your future steps too. We all too quickly accept what hindsight offers us as lessons and growth offered with precision and care, but fear that the same love won't exist in the future. We accept past abundance, and yet we buy into the idea of future scarcity. All we have to do is trust and have faith that our lives are filled with abundance. How could we ever doubt such a power? Is it that we don't believe it, or that we get too caught up in our own material desires that we lose sight of what is really happening? It is worth considering as we venture forward on our paths to growth and reconnection.

The second most important virtue is gratitude. We have all heard of different ideas and theories behind gratitude and the power it has in our world, and to one another. We can write a daily gratitude list in order to spend more time focusing on the positive and appreciating what we have in our lives instead of thinking about what we lack. There is a theory that states that when we look at life and give appreciation for what we have, even if we don't physically or emotionally have it yet, our physical self reacts by believing that we do. It believes that we have received that love; it believes that we are living that dream job; it believes that we are all that we know we will be. And we have the capacity to "trick" ourselves into believing that it has already happened. In the world of quantum physics, physicists believe that this has an effect in the quantum realm which changes the frequency around you and attracts it to your life. The belief is that gratitude is not only a state of mind and attitude, but it is also a physical state of being.

Thinking back on my own experiences, I recall when I was waiting to hear about moving to Abu Dhabi. I believed so wholeheartedly that I would get the opportunity to move. So much that even in the car on the way to work, I would stream the local radio station from the UAE. I pictured myself in that car overseas, imagining the feeling of going to my job, and the sense of living somewhere new and exciting that would come with it. I knew in my heart that it was mine, and I gave my entire being the opportunity, three months in advance, to start living it. As we have yet to create the scientific method to prove this in the world of mainstream science, I am sure skeptics say that it was sheer luck. But even the choice of believing in life in such a way affects our reality. It may have been that I intuitively knew I was moving, or that intellectually I knew that all the right dots were connected for me, but on the most basic level, living in a state of gratitude while waiting for the opportunity to come to life created a far more enjoyable reality for me, than wondering, being uncertain, and doubting in the abundance of my future.

The power of trust and gratitude are beyond the capability of our own language. If you were to sit with these words, try to really understand them, dissect them and put them back together, you would only get half of their power. Yet, for me, these two words are such a powerful force in
creating a life that truly matters, that all I can continue to do is trust and be grateful.

My Personal Formulas to Life
When it comes to my current personal formula for life, it is simple: Love is God, and service is prayer.

This is my new formula in life, and it resonates deeply with what I am learning and what I understand. How do I actively pray through the service I do? How do I continue to connect with God through the love that I show? How do I honor our universal source through using service to create in the name of love for mankind? This is what I ask myself. This is how I see an existence that brings ultimate joy and fulfillment. For those of you who look at this and think it is too far-fetched or unrealistic, I call bullshit, and I am going to be the bluntest I have been in this book. If you don't believe this to be true, you are being too rigid in your capacity to understand the world around you, and you are forcing those same rigid expectations onto your world. It is likely you are working from ego, and have too many conditions on what you determine love to look like. In essence, you have too many conditions on your conversation with God. Not "God" as we have been forced to understand

"Him" through the different teachings of men who have rewritten the powerful words of our prophets to suit their own control and desires. But God as a pure source of love and guidance. The same energy that you feel when you look at that person who you have decided to share your life with, or even that particular moment with, and you can feel it encapsulate you like the submersion of your body into the ocean. The energy you get when you are working on something with so much joy and care, it is as if the magic of that work is coming through you. The energy you have when you are living authentically in the present moment, and everything around you feels like it's buzzing with life.

If you believe that these simple words are too profound, or are reserved for only a select group of people in this world, then you are currently choosing not to see the incredible brilliance of the world around you and the reality awaiting you. You are presently choosing to opt for the "hell" rather than the "heaven." You are currently choosing your reality as it stands right now. The moment we realize that we can remove ourselves from the pain that surrounds us—the mentality that limits us, the tribulations that stop us—we access a world, a reality, which is far beyond even our wildest dreams.

If this does not resonate with you, then do me a favor and before you cast these words aside, just ask yourself this: "Am I living a life that resonates with the depths of my soul? A life that is my authentic, joyous, and most grateful self?" If the answer is in any part "no," then you have some of your own work to do. You are capable of more, you are worthy of more, you are a glorious reflection of your own God. You are love. Please don't let the rest of us miss out on sharing that with you.

THE SPIRITUALITY LESSONS

Spirituality is the culmination of all that we are in this human reality. It is the foundation for what makes our relationships strong, our service profound, our love sweet, and our life abundant. It is our connection with all that is beyond our human comprehension, and it is innately built within us. After all that we have discussed in this book, this is our biggest quest in life: to connect with our authentic spiritual selves. The more we delve within, the more we will learn both about ourselves and all that is around us. It is the job of each of us to seek more, question everything, share our light, and serve humankind. Don't allow the ego to get in the way of all that we are capable of becoming. And always allow those around us to shine bright in their own search for truth.

1. **Be Kind.**

After all of the examples offered, for me, this is a no-brainer. But, as I mentioned, this can be one of our hardest lessons to learn, and even tougher to maintain. But why should kindness be so tricky? It can sometimes be tricky to show kindness as it can be seen as weakness or misinterpreted as being polite. But what I have learned is that kindness is a sign of only one thing—strength. To be kind may mean to be vulnerable at first, but kindness is one of the most influential tools we have, and it is our duty in this lifetime to find the right balance of kindness in all that we do. Kindness can be as simple as the kindness of tongue when you speak to someone, or seeing an opportunity where a person may need help or advice, and asking if you can help. It takes less energy to be kind than it does to be rude, selfish, or angry. We should all give this a try more often.

2. **Find Your God, but Don't Have Blind Faith.**

The word and idea of God has unfortunately been tarnished for many people over the years, especially within the gay community. For too long, we have been told that we are not only an outcast, but the way in which we love is not in line with that of God. I say, don't listen to it! Listen only to the depths of your soul, and find your version of your own God—whatever that may look like. It may be a connection through the words of our Prophets, it may be your daily yoga practice, or it may be as simple as the service you offer to others. You can call it God, the universe, the stars, whatever you like. But find it. Find your God, listen to it, pray to it, and find the magic in a world where you can easily get lost.

However, in that search, do not have blind faith. For blind faith means to listen and trust without knowing. So seek beyond yourself and find a balance between both spirituality and science. For I have found that God lives within both of those worlds—not one or the other. Find your God and do it with every part of your being—spiritually, intellectually, emotionally. For we have departed from the days of blindly believing in what those around us say, and we need to step into a new era where we can seek for ourselves and ask for more.

3. **<u>Engage in Meaningful Conversation.</u>**
This matters. And this is part of the purpose of this very book. Meaningful conversation matters. Not just for intellectual stimulation, but for you spiritually too. This has been a driving force between where I was and where I am now. We need more meaningful conversation in our lives. Whether it is amongst friends, family, colleagues, random strangers—it doesn't matter. Idle talk offers you nothing, and has negative spiritual effects on your body that we are slowly beginning to uncover. Choose to be conscious of your words, and choose to learn and explore in daily conversation, rather than just be present. Every minute of the day, you have the opportunity to find something new and expand your understanding of all that is around us.

4. **<u>Find What Brings You Joy and Turn That into Your Purpose.</u>**
In my work with Blonde and Bear, I have met so many people who were profoundly seeking their purpose. They wanted something to be super passionate about. They have seen the hashtags and Instagram posts, they have watched their favorite TED Talk over and again, and they have decided that they want more. But then the most prominent issue arises for them—"What the heck is my purpose? And how do I find it?"

Well, I have come up with a simple formula that I like to suggest to clients, friends, and anyone else I am engaged with in this conversation. It may take some time, as we learned in the "Careers" chapter, but it is a surefire way to find it.

I. Seek what brings you joy. Even the simplest joy. Just find something that brings you joy when you do it. It could be writing, drawing, singing, making quilts, building websites… something.
II. Start doing it more often! As often as you can. See what you can do with it and where it takes you. If you start to lose the joy, that's fine; seek

something else. But once you find that a wildfire has been lit, keep it going.
III. Once your wildfire is ignited, this is what I like to call your "passion." Hurrah—you have found it! To find your passion simply means to find something that you have joy in doing over and again with the same excitement and care as the first time, if not more.
IV. Now, here comes the crucial part: Once you have found your passion, how do you turn this into purpose? It's quite simple, actually. It's through service. Take what you are passionate about and find a way to offer it as a service. It may not be life-changing. It may not be your big career move; in fact, it may just continue to be a hobby on the side. But take what you're passionate about and turn it into a service. This creates purpose. It may not be your ultimate life purpose, but it is a purpose for something fulfilling, something that will get you up in the morning, and something that others will benefit from. When you start to do this more often, you will find that your passions will grow, and your service to others expands beyond anything you ever imagined. We are social creatures with an innate desire for connection—what better way than to connect through passionate service in action?

5. <u>Your Reality Is Built on Your Own Perception.</u>

My final lesson is one that might not seem so powerful at first, or even might seem to just be a fact for some. But I want to reiterate this lesson that I learned. Our reality, all that is around us; our emotional responses, the color, the smells, the love, the hurt… all of it; this reality is built on our own perception. What we experience and how we experience it, is something that we have the power to control internally. Whether we want to be a victim or a superstar, whether we want to be kind or be vicious, or whether we want to see the world with love or offer it hatred. This reality is up to us.

The outside world may offer you difficulties; it may tell you that you are unloved, or worthless, or not capable, but it is up to us to decide to listen, to accept, and to create that world for ourselves. To put it in perspective, think back to five years ago. Where were you? What were you doing? And how did you think the world looked then? Now, look back two years ago. Do you remember the change that had occurred? Maybe you felt better, or perhaps you felt worse? Now, look at yourself at this moment. The reality you are in, the emotions you feel, the outlook you hold: Is it the same as that of the person you were two or five years ago? Of course not, certainly not in every aspect.

Whether we choose to accept change or not, it is inevitable. It occurs on a daily basis, in every waking (and sleeping) moment, and only those who fight it, find change to be the most difficult.

But during those changes, can you see how your view of the world has changed too? Maybe it is as simple as your relationship or perspective on money? Or perhaps you found love or lost it? The reality you once believed is no longer the reality in its entirety that you live in now. That is the power of perception. So rather than think that everything happens as a result of this thing called "life," what if you saw it as something you had the ability to use in order to create a reality that truly mattered to you? If you want more love, then look at life with loving eyes. If you want more kindness, then be kind and seek the kindness of others. If you crave to do more than you feel you are doing now, then stop sitting still in fear and find that change. Your reality is your perception. It's even called the theory of relativity in physics—one of the fundamental building blocks of this universe to which we are connected. Create the life you dream about—so that when you wake, you never want to go back to sleep.

REDEFINING PURPOSE

Throughout my life, I have been seeking this elusive thing called purpose. When I was a young child, it came in the form of my dream of being an archaeologist, or James Bond. Whichever came first. When I was in my early teens, I dreamt of being the next Brad Pitt or Hugh Jackman—basically, some famous actor who would live their life delivering stellar performances, signing autographs, and being rich and famous. When I was in my late teens, this changed to working in a highly paid and super important corporate job and traveling the world. By my early twenties, it escalated slightly and I still wanted to have a high paying corporate job and travel the world, but I would go between that idea and running my own not-for-profit (NFP) foundation. And underneath all of that, I just wanted to work for myself by the time I was thirty-five.

All of these ideas would come and go, and life happened in between it, but ultimately I was constantly seeking this "purpose" that I have found many of us are seeking in this lifetime. I had this idea in my mind that if I found this ideal job, or that ideal concept, then I could use it to live happily ever after. Maybe I watched too many Disney films when I was a kid, as I seem to see a theme of this "happily ever after" hindering my views in life! But what is this desire for purpose? What is this innate "itch" that I have had, and for the most part, many other people I have met have, that is yearning for us to find something of meaning in this lifetime? Is it that I need to find the perfect job in order to be happy? Or, like when I was a child dreaming of becoming James Bond, is this feeling just our childlike imagination at play?

Over the years, as I have described in this book, I decided to continue chasing that "itch." It is the theme of my book for a reason, and it saw me experience some of the most amazing things this world has to offer. But, so many times along the way, I felt let down, brokenhearted, or simply lost, when the "itch" I thought I had didn't translate into the reality I thought I wanted. But what is it about this purpose that I wasn't getting? I got those dream jobs, traveled the world, did development work in rural communities, wrote concepts for my own NFP foundations, and still, at the end of the day, had this yearning that wouldn't subside. I would literally get that "dream" job, and within six to twelve months be bored again, feel like I had been misled and that there was something better still waiting for me.

Well, what I have learned in my own pursuit of truth is that this yearning, this desire for more, this dream of the ultimate life purpose, this "itch," was always going to be on the horizon and never quite attainable in my current mind-set. Why is that? Well it had nothing to do with material realities but had everything to do with my own internal beliefs. Have you heard the saying—"Belief drives Behavior?" Well, this isn't some new age, life coach conversation around how your limiting beliefs are stopping you from your greatest potential, but rather that your very core beliefs could be the reason you feel you are lacking in purpose.

What do I mean by this? Well, two of my major themes in life have been spirituality and purpose. And as mentioned in the previous chapter, spirituality for me was a cup that was filled with old trinkets and flawed understandings. It was a space that I had yet to explore properly, and as such, allowed old beliefs to be the framework for my reality. Over the last two years, as I stepped into my thirtieth year, I decided to redefine what those systems looked like, and what I found was quite literally life changing. I believe that your beliefs, the framework you work in, are quite literally driving your daily behaviors. I always thought I was pretty driven and capable of achieving whatever I wanted, and this has been true in my lifetime. But the limitation came in that I was achieving things that were not progressive or ultimately of service to others all the time.

What I found is that my purpose was flawed, because my beliefs, my spirituality, didn't allow for me to understand what I was looking for. And once I started shifting my beliefs, my behaviors and my purpose began to shift too. Instead of walking through life with this desire for purpose and seeking it in material outcomes, I was able to find a deeper understanding of what it means, which has become my internal compass for purposefully creating a reality that truly matters to me. What I have learned is that purpose isn't about the actual momentum of what you are doing, as much as it is about the internal motor that is driving it.

When I speak about purpose, I am not just speaking about finding the dream job, I am also speaking about the bigger questions in life, like the age-old questions—Why are we here? And, what is the purpose of life itself? Now, I am certainly not saying I have those answers for you, and if anyone does say they have the final answer, I would suggest you step away from them and continue on your own investigation of truth. But I feel that through shifting the framework of my beliefs, I have finally found the right path toward my purpose.

So how did I find this path and where can each of us start in order to find it? Well, my first suggestion to finding your purpose is to look at one very important topic—Death.

What Can Death Teach Us about Life?
You are probably wondering why it has gone a little morbid, right? Well, that thought in itself may suggest that you need to ask yourself this question more than ever before. For me, finding my path toward a more fulfilling and purposeful life began when I asked myself this question. What did I understand or believe about "death"? What answer did I hold in my spiritual cup, that set the tone for my purpose in this lifetime? If beliefs drive behavior, then surely the answer to this final ending could be driving my own daily actions?

In my pursuit for truth, I came across a discussion within the Bahai writings, a spiritual source that I have found huge depth and insight in exploring, that sparked my interest and challenged me to my core. What if death was the same as birth? This topic intrigued me. For so many of us, we hear topics like this and, without being conscious of it, apply our preexisting beliefs against it and carry on. I could have done the same had I not been actively breaking down my own framework of beliefs—but I chose not to. This theory though has fundamentally changed my perspective on life altogether. And the reason for it, is that my previous belief on death was either limited to a world where we only have one chance anyway, so if we do good, then great, but if we don't, then we'll be six feet under soon so who cares? And the other view was along the lines of reincarnation, where I thought that we have this lifetime to get right, and hopefully come back again in a good place, or worse case, risk the next lifetime coming back as an ant or something. But either way, I had a choice and it wasn't too risky.

This isn't to say that people who hold these views are wrong or that they can't be true. Not at all. In fact, for many of us, what other views could we have outside of this or simply believing that we will go to "heaven" or "hell"? Our teachings have been limited for some time and so we have created lives based on these ideas. But without knowing it, we have underestimated how powerful these beliefs are when it comes to our daily practice and purpose. If I believe that this is one lifetime we have, so live large or die quietly, why would I have to find any reason to live a life of servitude, be kind, or seek unity? This is our only life! I am going to party, have fun, enjoy the material possessions of this reality, and live a life serving the most important person—me. On the other hand, if I believe that we either reincarnate, or go to a designated part of the sky or ground, dependent on our behavior, as outlined in understanding of spiritual writings, then that too dictates what type of world I want to create. I may offer myself in service more or reach out to others, but what is the driving force behind it? Is it from the kindness of heart, or is it obligation driven by the concept of an external God who will reprimand me like a parent does a child?

What if instead though, we delved a little deeper and tried to make sense of the concepts from a somewhat rational and philosophical perspective? What if death and birth are one in the same, this lifetime is part of many worlds, and there is a deeper purpose attached to it all? Here's an analogy that helps me make sense of this concept: An embryo is in the womb of its mother for nine months prior to being born. It has nine months to live in its safe and warm universe, and growing its physical faculties for the world it is about to enter. This we know. There can be complications, there can be factors that limit its growth if the mother is not healthy, but it's the only chance it has. In that nine months, the baby has to grow all of its physical faculties, in order for it to have the best chance it can in this world. For us, already in this universe, we look at the baby in the mother's womb and we wait with anticipation and love. We know what it is doing, we know the time we have to wait, and we hope that the baby is growing and developing everything it needs. Around the nine-month mark, something remarkable happens. The body of the mother knows that the baby has had enough time, and she gives birth, bringing this newborn in to our universe and ready to begin growing in the world. After coming into this world, the child grows into an adult, builds a life and family for itself, and then one day, it "dies." Leaving this universe and continuing into our many theories of death. Our emotional response is sadness, despair, and grief, as we, the humans, remain in this human experience, bound by space, time, and emotion.

Now, imagine it from the perspective of the embryo (if the embryo could have the capacity to understand what is happening in the same way we do). You are born into your world, it is large to begin, but over time you start to fill it up. You are warm and safe, and fed with love and sustenance from the creator of your universe. You hear noises and see sparks of dull light, but you disregard them as you are safe and warm. Every day you feel yourself developing—arms and legs forming, organs developing, body growing. You don't know why, but it is happening and you make sure you get the right things in order for it to happen. Suddenly, as time goes on, you begin to feel uncomfortable. You get restless and can't quite fit the space anymore. You wonder what will happen when you get too big for this universe, but you believe that this is it. One day, your life force breaks, your world begins to crumble, your universe is shifting rapidly, and you can feel yourself falling out of this comfortable space. Could this be death? I mean, it is death of this universe, so surely this is it? As your universe dies around you, the light is overwhelming and there is noise and sound and energies that surround you. The space you move into is enormous and you can't understand what is happening. Your previous life force of warmth and security disappears and something is waiting for you on the other side. What could this be? And then, you are born into the next universe.

Now, let's pause for a minute and start to think about this for ourselves. The embryo, even though we understand it to be what it is, does not know that the next universe is only a layer of skin away. It doesn't know that we are all cheering it on from the next universe, praying it builds those arms and legs, ready to be able to take on its duties in this world. It doesn't know that the universe it is within, the love that is waiting for it, and that its creation in this human form is partly due to you and your existence. It knows none of this, and we know all of it. Yet, in so many ways it experiences its own "death," only for us to call it "birth." In this universe, we see that embryo's death of its universe as a birth into our own. However, fast-forward our own reality and hit play at the time where we are ready to pass on from this human form into whatever is next, and we find we are doing the same thing—seeing death, instead of birth.

Why is it we automatically think it is the end of the road? Why is it that we believe death to be final, or to move us into a new home of eternity based on actions of this lifetime, or that we hit restart and come back again? And if we do believe in any of those frameworks, what does that mean for our purpose in this lifetime? This discussion goes on to say that, like the embryo in the womb whose purpose is to build physical faculties for this lifetime, to which we can all attest, the purpose of the human life is to build spiritual faculties for the next. And for us to see death, not as finality, but rather the transformation from one world into another.

All of a sudden, after grasping that idea for a while, I realized the profound impact that it has on my reality. If I continue to work within the constraints of the existing framework, where death is some form of finality or a shift into an unknown eternity, it is almost discouraging to pursue anything to do with it. In the same way as when I know I am at the end of something and I find it hard to stay focused, could it be that the very idea that we are at the end of a process limits our drive to want to explore deeper and further? Could it also be that the previous frameworks were relevant for the periods of time that they were offered, as human consciousness had not yet evolved, but we are now in a time of deeper understanding and growth?

For me, this very idea of removing finality, of removing death as the endgame, and of understanding that in this life we must grow and evolve our own spiritual faculties for the next universe, in the same way the embryo built its physical faculties for this one, shifted my entire outlook on life. This outlook, along with redefining my own spirituality, took me from viewing the world with fractured ideals that all seemed to end in finality, to seeing life as ever evolving and ever changing. Suddenly, my purpose of finding that perfect job, and finding that perfect place to live, and finding that perfect partner, shifted from the endgame, to being part of the even bigger equation where these were just part of the experience and not the required outcome. Through perceiving the world with a lens where our purpose is to continually grow spiritual faculties, my purpose shifted from a focus on self-serving, to a desire for service of others. It went from passing time in the pursuit of societal expectations to ensuring that I used my time effectively, to progress and build my spiritual faculties through service and connection to those around me, as well as through further education of the subject. Through this new outlook, I found that my beliefs, which drive my behavior—my spiritual understandings, driving my purpose—shifted to see the world through two new perspectives, progress and service.

The questions I began to ask myself more frequently in all that I do were: Is what I am doing of *service* to others? And does it assist me in my own *progress*, as well as in the progression of those around me?

Building Spiritual Faculties

Before we delve further into this concept of service and progress further, I want to hit the pause button again and move back to the main topic here, which is a life focused on building spiritual faculties. What does this mean and how do we live a life that creates a growth in our spiritual faculties?

Well, I think for everyone this may be different and will generate your own independent investigation of truth. In the same way that an embryo, who grows into an infant, is unaware of why it is experiencing this growth process but ensures it continues to take in all the nutrients it requires for its development, many of us within our own universe have a chance to do the same thing. For me, spiritual faculties are beyond our physical realm, and created from the same source as our soul. It is the effects though that we translate into physiological responses as humans that we can use to make sense. For instance, when I do *this*, it makes me feel *this*. And when I do *that*, it makes me feel *that*. We know when something makes us feel good or when we are in a space of progress, as much as we know those things that make us feel bad or have negative effects.

But so many of us spend our lives asleep or unconscious to the effects that some experiences, feelings, actions, even words, have on our own spiritual growth. In different parts of the world, we see kindness as weakness, while in others, we confuse politeness with an act of kindness or generosity. These can have profound effects on us in ways that I think we are limited to perceive. The human body was created with five key sensory perception tools—sight, sound, smell, touch, and taste. These sensors, alongside our innate spiritual instinct, allow us to be profoundly deep and aware creatures within our universe. Yet, for so many of us, we misunderstand the power of things that we can't necessarily perceive with those five sensory tools. If we can't see or feel it, physically, we then believe that it has no effect. But as our scientific data and research continues to evolve and expand, so does our capacity to perceive things that we once could not. Just because we can't make sense of it right now, doesn't mean it lacks the potential to exist.

For instance, consider the power of kind words. I am sure we have all been told that we need to speak kindly to others. In fact, this very teaching has been around since the time of Christianity, where Jesus said, "Do unto others as you would have them do unto you." And during the original times of Christianity, it was a new lesson for people who lived in a world that lacked not only in education, but also worked from a far lower capacity of consciousness, to which its society reflected. But despite these words having been around for so many millennia, we still can't seem to understand it within the human experience. In a world that is bound by information technology, we see more than ever the carelessness and hurt caused through the poor use of words. An average response from many people is that we should just ignore those who speak poorly and not worry about what is said. But could this lack of understanding actually have a profound effect on us from a scientific level? What if the words, which resonate and hold a specific energetic frequency, are actually lowering the capacity for growth within society?

Researchers have done studies using the power of words on plants, by getting two trees and surrounding them with speakers. They would play kind words on one tree and mean words on another. Within a few days, they found the effects to not only be profound but physically hurtful. The plant surrounded by kind words was visibly strong and vibrant, while the one surrounded by mean or degrading words visibly wilted and died. This was not a theory, this was real. And whilst I am sure we could battle with the many variances and factors involved in these tests, we don't have to go far to know that if we place ourselves in the positions of those trees, we can relate and feel the same effects ourselves.

Now, what does this say about our spiritual faculties? To me it says that we have factors in this universe that are beyond our current comprehension, which we do not understand, but that have far greater power and influence on our human state than we give credit for. The fact that for centuries we did not understand the words of a prophet, which has been repeated through every dispensation since, and yet our science is now proving the effects of some of those same words in our daily lives, tells me that we underestimate the power of our spiritual faculties.

So how do I see these faculties and what do they look like? To be more specific, I believe spiritual faculties are connected to our greatest human virtues. For instance, the power of kindness, empathy, or compassion, are all part of the tools we need to focus on, in order to grow those spiritual faculties. These things, whilst they are seen as somewhat emotive in the human state, as we measure the effects they have on our physiological self, have far more profound impact on our soul whether we can scientifically measure this yet or not. I believe, until we find a way to prove these factually, we see the effects in their attributes. When we are empathetic toward another, we remove opportunity for hostility, discord, and divide, and we connect with the person through that binary force we spoke about earlier—love. And in the same way we are finding that love is the very essence that could be the force that drives our entire existence, so wouldn't it be more beneficial for our growth to continue working on these virtues?

On the topic of human virtues, whilst we cannot necessarily study the effects it has on our soul from a scientific level, other studies have been conducted to identify human strengths within the landscape of Positive Psychology. This theory of Positive Psychology was a way for psychologists to develop programs that focused on what strengths we have, rather than what we believe we don't have, like most previous programs. An incredible study on this topic was undertaken and written about in a book called, *'Character Strengths and Virtues: a Handbook and Classification'*, by Christopher Peterson and Martin E P Seligman. It is more of a textbook than easy read, but definitely worth researching for yourself. From this study, researchers found twenty-four human strengths in character, which all corresponded to a set of key human virtues. To agree on the virtues in the first place, they studied all major religions and philosophical traditions, and found six classes of human virtues that were consistent across all faiths, traditions, and cultures. Those being: *wisdom, courage, humanity, justice, temperance, and transcendence*. Under each of these virtues, and through that focus on strength of character, they came up with twenty-four strengths that they believe define the human character. And the reason I loved this, whilst I can't share all of their findings in this book, is that these are character traits, virtues, that all of us hope to achieve in our lifetime.

For me, this study provided a great insight into the commonality of virtues across the world and what each of us is striving to achieve on a daily basis as humans. And whilst we could remain focused on it as a study of psychology, we certainly cannot underestimate the power that this holds, given it is based on the religions, traditions, and cultures of the entire world across millennia. Each country may be separated by distance, language, or cultural backgrounds which create external differences between people, but at the end of the day we are all human, all living in this same universal reality and bound by the same universal laws. Whether we see it or not, these types of studies continue to show us that we are all the same, and we all seek the same thing—a greater purpose. We try to achieve this purpose by unconsciously working on the human attributes of what I see as those spiritual faculties—our virtues. It could be that the more we can express ourselves through these character strengths, the more we can focus on a life bound by these virtues. And the more virtues we live by, the greater chance we have at living a more purposeful life.

I believe every day we have an opportunity to be able to grow or diminish these virtues, and it is up to each of us to decide what path we take. But how do we continue to grow these virtues? I believe it is quite clear; through daily action and working to our strengths. It is our responsibility to find a way to develop these strengths and virtues each and every day, and I believe the best way to do that is through service. For instance, if we were to look at the world around us, and instead of thinking, "What can I get out of this world for me?" we thought, "How can I serve those around me?" Imagine what type of world we would create. A world where each of us is battling on our own journey, but instead of sitting in that space and feeling that the world is against us, we actively chose to get up and help others instead, which, in turn, helps us. It's a win-win.

Creating a Life of Service and Progress

After some soul-searching and personal growth, listening to the different theories on life and death, and seeking a version of truth that aids me toward a flourishing life, I came to the realization that I need to focus on two important factors in everything I do—progress and service. No matter what I do, I now carry with me this new outlook which aids in making decisions and ultimately driving my behavior each day. Because remember, beliefs drive behavior. Whether I am looking at my relationships with friends or my significant other, career choices, social outings, education options, and even where I want to travel, I refer to this new personal guide.

If one of the main purposes of experiencing life is about building spiritual faculties, and those spiritual faculties are driven by the development of virtues, then I should always be looking to see whether I am fostering behavior to develop those virtues in my life. It begs the questions: Is what I am choosing to do allowing me to serve those around me? Is what I am choosing progressing me, and hopefully those with me, toward our ultimate purpose of growing our spiritual faculties?

If it is a yes, then I feel comforted to know that I am working within the boundaries of my most ideal life path. If it is a no, then I should not be surprised when it begins to all fall apart.

Now, this theory isn't just something that sounds interesting to me. I have found ways to begin testing it against the world around me in order to see if this is what others experience too. And one of my favorite comparisons I have made for myself takes us all the way back to the world of the atom. I will try to keep this as simple as possible, even for myself. For those who are science junkies and know all about the theories of quantum physics, you will understand the nature of the atom. The atom, for so long, baffled scientists as a very large unknown, with many unable to place its relevance in the world as previous scientific theories did not allow for it to exist in the way we understood reality to be. Despite this, the theory of the atom has been said to exist as far back as 440 BC when Democritus, a Greek scientist and physicist, wrote about it. However, by the nineteenth and twentieth centuries, a number of scientists took the previous theories and advanced them, to take our old standard physics theories and couple them with the new quantum theory that we understand today. The atom, on the most basic level, creates our entire reality. Atoms are the basic units of matter and the defining structure of all elements.

So how can the atom assist us in understanding progress and service on a deeper level? Well, as this basic unit of matter is what creates our entire universe, why not go back to the very beginning of all things, to try and understand whether, even at the most fundamental level of reality, we are trying to achieve the same thing as that which forms our universe.

What has occurred in order for this reality to exist in the first place? And could it be that it is the same process that takes place, all the way from the atoms coming together, to the creation of entire human civilizations? Just like in my previous topic of spirituality, where we touched on "Love: our most divine source," could it be that the same binary force of love, and the rules behind that force, are present even within the human experience? Could it be that we are not using our scientific knowledge and our philosophical views of this reality to gain a deeper insight on what our deepest human desires mean? We are a fusion of spirit and matter after all, so could it be that the answers lie in the crossroads of these things?

Here's an example of what I mean: to make breathable oxygen, the most fundamental requirement of our existence, we require two atoms to come together to form the O2 structure. That is, we need two atoms of oxygen to form a molecule in order to create the air we breathe. Whether they are conscious of it or not, these atoms bounce around in our atmosphere and have two options in their existence—form with other atoms that do not sustain life, or bond with another oxygen atom through the binary force of nature and have the potential to serve humanity (support life on Earth). Whether this is through a consciousness we don't understand or simply through the binary force of "love" in nature, the action takes place and it is what forms our reality. It is how we breathe, how the human body is formed, and how an inconceivable number of creatures exist in this world. This bond is, quite literally, the reason behind how things are formed in this universe and come into existence.

So could it be that this same force—the one that brings atoms to bind with one another in order to form molecular structures of the most fundamental compounds of our existence—those molecules continue to form up the line of creation until we see the infinite universe that surrounds us? This is the same force that creates our "itch" that we experience in our human lives. Could they all be connected? And could it be that this feeling of purpose is the same "feeling" (if small chemical atoms could understand complex and highly-formed human senses of emotion) that the atoms that bound to one another, that ultimately created our existence, felt when they came into existence themselves?

For some, this may be a little far-fetched, and I am not a physicist myself obviously, but what a philosophical theory allows is an opportunity for us to try and see things from a different perspective. It allows each of us the opportunity to realize that maybe we aren't as divided and segregated as we once believed, and that, in fact, the desires we feel are from the same force that created the reality that we live in. And that if it is the same force that created our own reality, then it is a requirement of each of us to find a way, like those building blocks of atoms, to come together to seek our most progressive and serving partners, and to create unity in order to build on what is already in existence.

In so much of our spiritual text, I read about how we must find a collective consciousness, and that we are moving into a time where we must find a way to come together. Could it be that we are coming to understand that without this unity, this collaboration between the different "elements" of our society, we will limit the capacity for growth in our world? Could it be that we are speaking the truths that are innate with us, driven by this life force we have yet to define but currently call "love," and all for the same purpose as the energy that forms our physical reality in the first place—that is, progress and service to something greater than the original element itself?

This insight, while deeply philosophical, has changed my outlook on this "itch" that has been with me from the very beginning. An "itch" that was a desire to seek progress, to find a deeper purpose in what I do each day, and to continue to serve those around me. This "itch" has shaped the way I see the world, the decisions I have made, and the opportunities I have sought. But it has also been part of my biggest challenges. There have been many times when all I wanted was to make something happen that looked good in my mind, even if it didn't align with those desires and rather just aligned with my ego. Times where I have looked at work to do, people to date, and things to buy, that served no one other than me. This challenge was not about whether it is right or wrong, because at the end of the day my life is what I make it, but it is about what aligns with my most authentic self and what will progress and serve beyond myself. When I made those decisions to follow my own vain imaginings, I found that I felt most distant from that "purpose" I so deeply desired. Whether it was chasing my dream corporate job that was driven by money and role title; dating that guy that was the most handsome man I have ever seen, but had not a great deal more going for him or simply didn't align with my own true values; or buying that item that I didn't need, couldn't really afford or that ultimately brought about a momentary glimpse of an emotion called happiness. These were all part of that battle with this innate desire.

To add further perspective to this theory and with the belief that we are all achieving something greater than ourselves, let's look at the human body and how it functions. To begin, imagine society as a human body and every person within society as a cell in that body. Now picture that body diseased, meaning that body is at DIS-EASE with its most flourishing self. The function of all the internal organs, the blood that pumps through its veins, the hair follicles, the nervous system, the skin… All of it is exacerbated in some capacity as a result of this dis-ease. In order to begin the healing process, the cells in the body have a decision to make—come together to heal or remain stagnant and die. Every one of those cells in that body knows this innately and has a responsibility to come together, within its own group of collective cells to heal the body. The kidney cell doesn't sit idly listening to the stories being shared by the central nervous system of the trauma taking place, and panic that there is nothing it can do to heal every part of the body, so therefore just does nothing. Nor do the skin cells in the foot sit back and think that the cells of the fingernails are going to come down and heal the pain that falls within the remit and responsibility of their part of the body either. The hair follicles don't believe that their job is to heal the liver, nor do the blood cells believe they are responsible for finding a healing solution for the mucus membranes in the mouth. Actually, they may have some effect on it, but their primary focus is to heal based on their primary purpose—which is to clean the blood of toxins and create new healthy cells to fight off the bad ones. Every single cell in that body knows that they have a job to do and that they have to find a way to heal the space in which they live. The skin cell knows that if it comes together with other skin cells, it may not heal the entire body of its disease, but rather it may just heal that one cut on the arm that is causing aggravation to the healing process of the body. The liver cells know that if it focuses on finding its cell tribe, it can come together and begin creating new liver cells and enhance its function within the overall body system. Every one of those cells has an innate purpose, fueled by the binary force of love, to come together and serve something greater than itself. And if each of those cells decided it wasn't their responsibility, then the body would continue to degrade and eventually die. But if they acknowledge that the "itch" they feel is the same feeling of the elements that formed to create the cell in the first place, then they would know that something bigger is in motion.

I believe, as the souls connected to the human body, we are no different. We are all cells of a bigger function and we all have an innate desire of purpose—to find ways to serve beyond the capacity of our self. This isn't some mystical tale of theology or something you read in a self-help theory. This is seen in the nature of our material existence. It is all around us. Yet, we seem to ignore it and believe we are separate to this process, when it is taking place in our very own bodies right now. In the oxygen we breathe, the body functions are keeping us alive and our souls are shining as a reflection in a mirror in this human experience.

With this in mind, and working from the theory that we require progress and service in all that we do, then what decisions would you make differently in your life? What can you see already that you know is not serving you or anyone near you? And what have you allowed in your life that isn't progressing your own development and the development of the greater "body" of mankind? Is that relationship you keep going back to the same as the two atoms that come together and form breathable oxygen? A relationship that is a result of the binary force of love and created to serve and progress? Or have you taken your atom of oxygen and created a compound that can't sustain life? One that would have come together through this same force, but in the spectrum of human flourishing, has the potential to be destructive and harmful.

Is that career you are giving every part of yourself to, serving your community, your own development of your spiritual faculties, and progressing mankind? Or is it toxic and harmful, self-serving, and time wasting? Are you the kidney cell floating aimlessly in the diseased body, distant from the organ to which you provide life? Or are you finding ways to be used for healing and support?

To ensure that we are living a life of purpose, we have to find ways to understand our function within the world and how we can best serve the greater body in which we live. We have to decide on what our core beliefs are, what they stand for, and who they stand for, in order to understand whether we are living in alignment to our most authentic self. Like the skin cell who knows its function in the world, we, too, have to find our own path. I believe that by constantly refining this search, we are making the most progressive decisions to guide us toward a life of human flourishing and service.

The End of Finality

Whether it is the doomsday movie, the science seeker, or the religious extremist trying to prove a point, we are all obsessed with seeking finality. Even in our very idea of death we seek the need for finality. But what I have offered here is something different. And what I want to offer is another way to look at the world—Stop seeking finality! What I have learned when it comes to seeking purpose is that once I removed this idea of a final outcome, my world became so much more fluid and filled with potential. The sheer anxiety I felt when I was trying to find *my ultimate purpose* still gives me heart palpitations. I used to think that purpose meant the answer to why we are here; the ideal job; the perfect partner; the right house; the best car; the most amazing life. But what I realized is that these were all vain imaginings. These were not reality, but some strange expectation or warped view manifested from past behaviors. What I have learned though, and this goes even further past the idea of purpose, is that finality does not exist.

Instead, life is an ever-evolving theory—a sphere of potentiality where truth can be found in the ever-present reality in the form of theories. Even this book, my current ideas and lessons, can only be seen really as truth with a small "t." Truth with a capital "T" can exist (meaning what we truly believe to be "truth"), but it is dependent on perspective. To give you an example of what I mean, let's look at the idea of a progressive revelation. For some people, this very concept may be confusing but bear with me as I try to explain my understanding. Within the Bahá'í faith, it is said that we live in a world where we have Progressive Revelation. That means that each Prophet came down, one after another, to offer progressive spiritual advice to the world of mankind. Meaning Abraham, Krishna, Moses, Zoroaster, Buddha, Christ, Muhammad, The Bab, Baha'u'llah, and many others in the lineage of time are all connected. Personally, I really appreciate this perspective as it appeases my rational mind, especially with hindsight and the ability to link many faiths together. But that is beside the point. What this very concept has offered to those seeking spiritual depth is that it breaks down the very concept of what is "truth" in that of a final answer. For instance, during the time of Jesus Christ, the world was offered a way to live—religious laws and concepts to advance mankind. These were truth, with a capital "T," during the dispensation of that Prophet. However, when Prophet Muhammed came, he brought with Him new laws and spiritual concepts that were right for that period of time. So it could be said that the truths of the previous dispensation were now a lowercase "t" and the new laws were truth with a capital "T." See where I'm going with this? Now this continues on, right through to where we are today. But it even means, with this new perspective, that the truths we are offered today, whilst they are relevant for the advancement of mankind in today's time period, if we were to see the world on a time line, and move outward so that the perspectives we see aren't those of today, but rather those of, say, three thousand years in total. It could be that all "truths" have a lowercase "t"—meaning they hold some truth but not truth in its entirety. They are not the final truth, for the truth is relevant to the perspective of the time. Kind of like the theory of relativity for those people who see the world through science.

Now, moving away from religion and into the world of science, we see the same thing. How many "facts" that existed, say only fifty to one hundred years ago, are today found to be superseded by a new fact or truth that we have come across through advancement in our scientific methods. Plenty! Whether it is to do with exercise regimens, synthetic drugs, cancer research, or the extent to which our universe is structured, what we once believed as "fact" (capital "F"), can very quickly change in our evolution. The reason this is so important when it comes to our own purpose is that we too often believe that this "finality" that doesn't exist elsewhere, exists in our own reality. But it doesn't! It is all a progressive theory. And the moment we fully grasp that concept, we are offered the ability to begin to take greater risks, seek bigger achievements, find different ways to explore the world, and investigate our own version of truth. I believe that once we accept that everything is a theory, that the truth is ever-evolving, and that purpose is a "progressive revelation," the sooner we will stop fear from holding us back and start seeking our own version of truth with childlike curiosity.

I believe purpose is not some final answer, some perfect job, or some ideal state. It is the drive we need to ensure that we are serving effectively and finding ways to progress ourselves and those around us. And that, for me, is the capital "T" truth of it all.

THE PURPOSE LESSONS

This is the last of my lessons, but certainly not the least. Purpose is a common theme and was part of the reason for this book. The "itch" was about chasing purpose, that sense of authenticity, that desire for progress and elevation. It continues to be a space where I am constantly attuning myself to listen to what I need and what those around me need. It is my shining light that only gets brighter through a more authentic connection with myself and my version of God. It is what gets me out of bed, keeps me up late at night, and has me leaning into some of life's most difficult situations. Purpose is what we are all seeking, and it is our job to decipher our own formula and find a way to put it into action.

1. **Be of Service.**
I have spoken about service throughout my book, and for good reason. We are in a time now where thoughts, words, and actions matter, more than ever. We have access to resources and people at the click of a button, and we have a daily choice between waking every day and living selfishly, or offering ourselves in service to those we are connected with. Service is as simple as seeing the light in another and finding a way to create an opportunity for them. It is as simple as offering to help your family or someone close with a matter that needs attention but may only be important to them. It is finding work in a field that may not be the most enticing for your ego, but that which brings you joy and offers your talents to others. Service is finding the gem deep within you and allowing mankind to reap its benefits. It is something we should do on a daily basis; it is the way we refuel our soul; it is the way we move our humanity forward, and it is our most significant connection and homage to our eternal source and creator.

2. **Seek Progress.**
Life is all about action. Gone are the days of sitting idle and thinking about how the world can change. It is about seeking progress in what we do through constant action. That doesn't mean working ourselves to a point where we are of no service to anyone, but rather tackling every situation with a mindset to find growth and improvement. *Progress* has two definitions: "Forward or onward movement toward a destination," or " Development toward an improved or more advanced condition." These could not sum up this lesson more perfectly. In life, we need progress. We feel our worlds rushing rapidly forward and we know that our time on earth is finite. Rather than watch those days drift by, limiting ourselves by believing in stagnant or idle thoughts, or doubting that we have anything to contribute, I implore each person to step up and take action in all that he or she does. I have learned that the only way we will continue moving toward a more prosperous world, whether it be the

world around us, or the world within, is with a focus on progress.

3. Never Ignore the "Itch."

I have written it over and again throughout this book, but this has been one of the biggest lessons for me. The "itch"— the feeling that something isn't right, that something better is waiting, that something bigger is possible. These feelings matter. It's not that I am not willing to settle for what I have; I am always grateful for what the universe offers me, but I am always eager to find new things to learn, explore new parts of the world, and challenge myself in ways that I have not previously been challenged. I have learned that the "itch" is part of my universal language. It is how I understand my next steps without the need for some clairvoyant. It is how I know what opportunity to pursue and what to leave alone. And it is how my "future-self" shows me what I need to focus on in the "now." Our "itch" is our most authentic self, speaking up in a voice that many of us don't yet understand or don't always listen to. In a world where we are bombarded with white noise and distraction, it is our duty to find some space, listen to that voice, and try to make sense of it for ourselves. Because on the other side of that voice, a life of purposeful adventure is waiting for every soul.

ITCH

A NEW VISION

So, where do I stand now with all of these experiences and lessons? At thirty years of age, what answers do I have? How do I now perceive the world? What does it mean to search for your authentic self?

For me, it means finding out where I stand in the spectrum of the world and constantly finding ways to expand and evolve. When it comes to the gay community, at first I was overwhelmed and confused with where I was meant to be, who I was meant to be, and how I was meant to express myself. But over time, I began to settle into my new skin and return back to the place where I felt most comfortable. Sexuality is not at the forefront of my personality. It wasn't a way that I previously represented myself to the world and how I engaged with people that I met. For some people, this may be how they choose to identify themselves. But I feel for many young people, this is part of the most significant discord that comes with "coming out." I believe you should own your sexuality in the same way you own other identities of yourself, but don't allow it to pervade or define you.

In this same space of the LGBT+ community, we are finally seeing in parts of the world that the hard work and dedication that went into standing up for the rights of our community, from our brothers and sisters of earlier generations, have started to pay off. We are seeing laws changing around the world, prejudices and discriminatory acts *slowly* decreasing, and the sun of the future, where love is allowed to be just that—love—creeping its way over the horizon. Now, I am not naive to know there is more work to be done, a lot more work, but what is the point of all of this hard work if one cannot feel celebrated and live joyfully in those progressed spaces, while continuing to build on it in different ways.

To understand what I mean, I will use an analogy that assisted me in understanding how I perceive the road ahead, and that is *growing plants from sand beds*. Generally, sand isn't a good growth medium for growing plants, unless it's composition is changed so that it can foster life. To me, our societies have been on a nutrient rich sand bed when it comes to LGBT+ rights. We had two options—one, we could leave it as it is, to the untrained eye, believing that it is simply sand and nothing can grow. Or, two, we could know that sand has the potential to foster life, do our best to cultivate that sand through changing it's capacities and structure, and try and grow plants from it. The people fighting for our rights are these cultivators. They have been our garden warriors, standing up for the right to love who we want to love, and using their own garden gloves to fight to make it happen. And over time, it has happened. In the enormous and rich sand bed that is society across the world, we are finding patches of green grass beginning to form. We are seeing rich soil bring life and the sand is changing into a prosperous garden bed. This very reality is incredible and we haven't seen it in our history before. But now that this garden bed of society is growing in patches and we are seeing grass patches of love come to life, it seems we are not quite sure what to do next. We see all the other remaining sand left to cultivate, and we are using our old ways to do that, plus some new gardening techniques we learned along the way, but we are uncertain what to do next with our new grass patches. If we don't look after them though, this now living soil will be left as it is and will miss it's opportunity to give more life.

So, what else could we do to this soil in order to give life to something more than grass? Put simply, if Stonewall began the modern-day process of turning sand into soil, which now provides life to grass, could we cultivate that same soil to give life to bigger plants or even a tree? Well, I believe, instead of just focusing all of our energies on cultivating that sand into soil in the areas where it still needs work, we need to also continue working on cultivating the soil in those rich grass patches so that it can foster even greater life.

Getting us to where we stand today comes from years of oppression, abuse, and disunity. It comes from people literally putting their lives on the line, to stand up and be heard. It comes from our desire, like many other minorities in the world, to have people in society remove their prejudices and discrimination, and allow us to have the same rights as many others were born with—despite how ludicrous that sounds. It comes from the need for justice and freedom. But it also now comes with a responsibility for the work done and for the future generations to come. We need to show respect, not only through appreciation of what has been done, but through our own work on what needs to be done for the future. For me, this comes in accepting that some of us may have been blessed to be born into the green patches of our community, and knowing that with this blessing comes responsibility. One that requires us to no longer be owned by the old stigma of sexuality, to find a connection to our authentic selves, to find our purpose, to find our own versions of God, and to be leaders in a divided and broken world. We have to own where we have come from, but more importantly step boldly toward the future, so that our own younger generations never have to even have a "coming out." I believe that the power we each hold after dealing with our own difficulties and adversities in coming to terms with our authentic self, gives us an advantage in being the leaders of tomorrow for our community. The work will not end here, but a bigger vision approach, a diversified community, and a desire to focus on further cultivating your patch of grass, knowing what the whole landscape requires, is what will take us to the next level.

When it comes to our individual stories, regardless of sexuality, I believe finding your authentic self is about chasing that "itch" of your own and discovering the balanced version of who you are deep down. It isn't about pursuing what the trends are, or what people expect of you. It is about battling through the places that need most of your attention to shift and change the way you see the world. Whether it is the relationship you have with yourself or your partner, the relationship you have with sex and your sexuality, the career you create in pursuit of a purpose, the experiences you have through travel, or the depths of your own spiritual being, it is up to you to seek more. So many of us sit idle in fear of what we do not understand, while the universe—God—offers us the opportunity to understand and develop ourselves further through different signs in life. It is our job to read them and follow the path. For those of us who have been comfortable with our sexuality for some time now, we need to make sure that we don't become complacent in the search for our authentic self. If you believe you have found it, and yet you still feel troubled or disconnected, I am going to say that you still have some more discovering to do. People before us have fought for years for our right to be equal. And still, to this day, we continue the good fight to ensure that those around are safe and protected to be who they were born to be. But now is the time to seek equality through perception. It is a time where we need to shift people's mind-sets through affirmative action and through breaking down stereotypes. We are responsible for the world we want to create, and we can begin to create it by finding and becoming our authentic selves.

What I have learned over the last thirty years is that life is all about balance. Balance in who we are, what we do, and how we do it. It is about seeking our highest self. It is about how we are more than only one version or quality of ourselves. It is about how spirituality is the basis for all that we do, and how we need to find our God. It is about how we may think that time delays what we want but in fact it is the lessons and experiences that we are waiting for. It is about how relationships matter and our integrity in them is vital. It is about how sex is not who we are. It is about finding our purpose through serving others. It is about how creativity is one of the most important outlets for people and yet still so underrated. It is about seeking experience to broaden your mind and your perspective—for that is all we have and all that creates our reality. Specifically for the LGBT+ community, it is about how some of us are now in a position where we can move beyond our pain bodies, or painful memories of the past, and start setting ourselves up for the future. It is about how we need leaders within our community to show everyone that we are more than just the sexual diversity of our people. It is about how we need to become conscious of our places in the world and start giving ourselves in service more than indulging ourselves in empty pleasure.

At thirty, I have learned that we are in the middle of an exciting roller coaster that is life, and it is each of our responsibilities to make of it what we can. Because if you do not make something of it, no one else will be responsible but you. This isn't a quote from some lame spiritual meme seen on the internet—this is a truth of our existence, and in a world of technology and the constant stream of information, it becomes harder and harder to be able to decipher this, but we must continually try.

If I were to one day wake up and have an incredible power where I could help to make a change in this world, it would be to help shape a better future for our younger generations, so they could progress even further than where we stand today. I would create a world where young men and women, especially those who identify as gay or lesbian, wake to a world where they are not only accepted for who they are sexually, but are also celebrated for every aspect of who they are. A world where we work together as a global community to continue seeking equality in its deepest form. Where we don't have to even have the term "come out." Where healthy and prosperous relationships were plenty, and our sexual diversity was not only celebrated, but also intellectual, spiritual, and emotional well-being and diversity were all equally celebrated amongst people. Where spirituality was actively part of our daily lives, and we found peace, security, and unity in our own versions of God. Where we sought after joy with priority and turned those joyful activities of the soul into purposeful service for one another—choosing to work toward love and unity. I would create a world where the ideals of the past generations, who did the best they could with the knowledge and power that they had, shifted and developed freely with the new wave of powerful, inspiring, and open-minded young people coming into our world. My vision is for all the other young "Lukes" out there to come into a world where you can love and be loved freely. Where spirituality and science are fundamentally part of your everyday understanding of the world, in equal measure. Where society values meaningful dialogue over backbiting and empty conversation. And where an entrepreneurial and creative purpose is admired the same as that of our most valuable intellects and scholars in society.

For me, this world already exists, but I have to work every day on creating it. Every day I have to make a conscious decision to focus on the light, move toward the ever-changing and ever-evolving vision of the world—fostering joy, love, and service in all that I do.

What type of world do you want for your tomorrow? What kind of world do you want for your children's tomorrow? We are all connected, and we are all responsible for what this reality looks like—both for ourselves and for each other. I implore you to chase your "itch"; find out more about who you are, what you want, and how the world can be better served by you. For each of us is on our own journey, and yet, we are all connected to one another. It is our responsibility to break the old laws of time and create a new space where we are equal, where we can love freely, and where we can serve one another, through the consistent development of our own characters. For we are more than the constraints of our current existence, and more than the words in which we offer the world. We are all creators, and we are all our version of God. Follow that "itch," even if it is small, as it is the guide that you need to find the greatest version of you.

ITCH

ABOUT THE AUTHOR

Luke Evans, like so many other young gay men in Australia, grew up believing he was different. Living in a culture formed through deeply engrained prejudicial views, he battled with loneliness and increased uncertainty, and believed that he didn't fit in the mold of what was 'right'. After spending years living and working abroad, exploring his identity, connecting with people from across global communities, and delving into his own spiritual truths, he has written his first full-length book at the pivotal age of 30. A coming of age story that uncovers his deepest lessons of authenticity, pays homage to those that came before him and yearns to be a beacon of hope and insight for people traversing their own paths.

www.ingramcontent.com/pod-product-compliance
Lightning Source LLC
Chambersburg PA
CBHW020323010526
44107CB00054B/1949